Understanding the *I Ching*

Understanding
the *I Ching*

CYRILLE JAVARY

Translated by Kirk McElhearn

Shambhala
Boston & London
1997

Shambhala Publications, Inc.
Horticultural Hall
300 Massachusetts Avenue
Boston, MA 02115
http://www.shambhala.com

9 8 7 6 5 4 3 2 1

First Edition

Printed in Canada
⊗ This edition is printed on acid-free
paper that meets the American
National Standards Institute
Z39.48 Standard.

Distributed in the United States by Random House, Inc.,
and in Canada by Random House of Canada Ltd

Library of Congress Cataloging-in-Publication Data

Javary, Cyrille.
    [Le Yi jing. English]
    Understanding the I ching/Cyrille Javary; translated
by Kirk McElhearn.—1st ed.
        p. cm.
    ISBN 1-57062-227-2 (pbk.: alk. paper)
    1. I ching.   I. Title.
PL2464.Z7J38 1997
299′.51282—dc21   96-52862
                                                                    CIP

Contents

Translator's Preface

When I first met Cyrille Javary, in Paris in 1985, he was just setting up the Centre Djohi,[1] which is a center for studying and exploring the *I Ching*. He had been studying the *I Ching* for a dozen years, and had studied Chinese, first in Paris and later in Taiwan, in order to better understand the workings of this text. A few months later Cyrille Javary asked me to help create a journal, *Hexagrammes,* and we have been working together on the *I Ching* ever since.

The book you are now reading, the author's second, was written in 1989 as an introduction to the *I Ching* for the general public. His first book, *A Study on the Origin of the I Ching,*[2] was a historical analysis of the *I Ching,* written for an audience of sinologists.

With this second book, however, he wanted to show just how important the link between theory and practice is. The sinologists look at the *I Ching* as just another classical Chinese text, while its evolution cannot really be examined without looking at its practical use. This book found its place in France, since the only other books available about the *I Ching* at the time were just translations of the *I Ching* itself.

There had been no attempt to understand the *I Ching*, and particularly no attempt to examine it in light of its historical context and its practical use. This book does just that, and I hope this translation will find a similar place in English-speaking countries, where translations of the *I Ching* abound, but, as in France, few works explain the *I Ching*.

One reason for this scarcity is that most people who write about the *I Ching* do not know the Chinese language and therefore have no access to the great wealth of material, both ancient and modern, that examines the *I Ching*.

Since this book was published, Cyrille Javary has written a number of articles for journals and magazines, published two other books, cotranslated two books about the *I Ching*, one from English and one from Chinese, and is now working on a new translation of the *I Ching* with extensive commentaries, the first such translation in French in more than a century.

A number of other things have happened concerning the *I Ching* since the publication of Javary's book. Important archeological discoveries have been made and many new scholarly books published that have changed the way one may look at the subject. But the story of the *I Ching* is still far from complete. Piecing together the evolution of this text is like doing a very large jigsaw puzzle with only half the pieces.

Because of this new information, a number of changes have been made to the text of the present book in order to correct or update information about the *I Ching*'s history, and a new conclusion has been written. The author would particularly like to thank Steve Moore for his helpful comments and Marie-France Benini for rereading and correcting the translation.

This translation was done with the author looking over my shoulder throughout, either in person or in spirit. We went through the entire manuscript together many times and discussed almost every sentence together. It was, as always, a great pleasure to work together.

Kirk McElhearn

Introduction

> That which releases things from their torpor
> and makes them move is called continuity.
> That which gives them another form while ad-
> justing them according to others is called
> change. That which raises them up to make
> them accessible to all men on earth is called
> the field of action.
>
> —*I Ching*, Great Commentary[1]

When the Marquis of Tai left for his long journey into the hereafter, he took along the two most valuable books of his time: the *Tao te Ching* and the *I Ching*. When his tomb was discovered twenty-two centuries later, the books were still there, written in black ink on long bands of silk. These two books are still, as then, the two pillars of Chinese thought.

In spite of its mysterious depth, the *Tao-te Ching*, the master work of Taoism, is familiar to us, if not entirely accessible. But the *I Ching* has remained in the abyss. Its symbols can be seen on the covers of the finest works of Chinese philosophy, but few authors do more than simply point out its importance

I CHING

I Ching

I: The meaning of this word can be understood by looking at the ideogram. It is divided into two parts: above, 日, the sun, and below, 勿, the evocation of liquid falling; the sun and the rain. The first meaning of I is related to changing weather, the change from sunshine to rain and from rain to sun. The general idea of change, transformation, comes from that. But this character also has two other meanings. The first is "easy," "simple," "natural." In the eyes of the Chinese, the essential quality of change is to be the very fluctuation that life is made of. The second derivative meaning is "stable," "firm," "rule." It may seem somewhat of a paradox for the same ideogram to mean both "change" and "stability." The *I Ching* itself explains this. It says that the only thing that is permanent is that everything always changes. *Change* is the only firm *reference point*, the only *natural* rhythm that can be made into a reasonable *law:* "The four seasons are constantly changing and transforming, and in this manner the annual cycle is constantly realized" (*I Ching,* hexagram 32, Commentary to the Judgment).

Ching: The underlying structure, both in the human body, such as the meridians of acupuncture, and in the body of knowledge of a civilization. This is the general name given to all the "master texts," such as the *Tao-te Ching,* "The Classic of the Path (Tao) and of Efficient Virtue (Te)" It can be used to describe books that are not philosophical (e.g. *Nei Ching,* "The Internal Classic," the master text of Chinese medicine) or even Chinese (e.g. Shen Ching, "The Holy Classic," the Bible). The literal meaning of this character is "warpage" (the threads stretched out lengthwise in a loom that give structure to the fabric that is woven), "longitude," "rule," "norm," "experience."

as one of the foundations of Chinese thought. It is the phantom of sinology.

Yet the *I Ching* is not an insignificant text. The name of this great book of yin and yang is *The Classic of Change*. Since the time when the Marquis of Tai lived (around 168 BCE), its place in Chinese civilization has been unequalled by any other work. It would be difficult to find a text that holds the same importance in Western civilization. The Bible has a similar venerability, and some of the works of the ancient Greek and Roman philosophers present fundamental ideas in the same manner, but no one text combines both of these characteristics.

How could such a text have been ignored in the West for so long? The answer is simple: the *I Ching* is considered to be a work of divination. The book is said to be "a means of understanding, even controlling, future events."[2] One might as well call it a book of fortune-telling, a superstitious relic of prelogical thinking that could not interest any sensible person in the twentieth century.

Nevertheless, the *I Ching* has interested many people, and sensible people at that. I. M. Pei, the architect who designed the recent additions to the Louvre Museum in Paris, and in particular the glass pyramids in its courtyard, has been a member of the French Academy of Beaux Arts since 1984. He closed his inception speech with a quote from *The Classic of Change* (which is the epigraph at the beginning of this chapter).[3] The Nobel prize–winning biologist François Jacob, in an article entitled "Analysis of Linguistic Models in Biology,"[4] suggested that his colleagues explore the *I Ching* in order to discover the principles they had not found in linguistics that are needed to fully explain the process of genetic coding. Fritjof Capra has cited its relationship to modern physics.[5]

Mention should also be made of artists such as the composer John Cage or the choreographers Merce Cunningham and Carolyn Carlson, who have based many of their works on the ideas of change and chance events that they discovered in the *I Ching*.

One cannot forget the Swiss psychoanalyst Carl Gustav Jung, who saw in the *I Ching* the most profound example of his theory of archetypes, as well as a model for explaining his ideas on synchronicity.[6] But one should also consider all those who use the *I Ching* to find practical solutions to personal or professional problems. These people refine their decision-making process by dint of the advice given in this amazing book of active wisdom. In China they can be counted by generations, while in the West they are without doubt counted by millions. But we are kept from understanding the experiences of the

Chinese because of their language, and of Westerners by a certain sense of shame. Fortune-telling! That is what most people think the *I Ching* is for. Because of this opinion, it remains, as a nuclear physicist working at the CERN in Switzerland said, "a charming intellectual mistress whom we are ashamed to be seen with in public."

The goal of this book is not to explain the *I Ching* to those who already know it but to give those who are interested some new information (chapter 1) and to discuss its history and importance in China (chapter 2), its current importance as a tool for decision making (chapter 3), and the perspectives that it opens up regarding chance (chapter 4).

The reader will also find, at the end of this book, a glossary of the specific terms used, an appendix listing the names of the sixty-four hexagrams, and a bibliography of selected books on the *I Ching*.

Understanding the *I Ching*

1

Hexagrams and Holograms
Getting Started with the *I Ching*

Rising and falling constantly, the lasting
and changing lines enclosed by a law. It
is change that is at work here.

—*I Ching*, Great Commentary,
Part 2, chapter 8 § 1

The *I Ching* is really a very small book. The core text,[1]
in Chinese, consists of only about four thousand
characters and would fit on one page of the *Peoples
Daily*.[2] If the official commentaries (the Ten Wings),
which are about six thousand characters long, were
added to this, a complete edition of *The Classic of
Changes* would take up only about thirty pages of the
book you are now reading. This is the foundation on
which the essence of Chinese philosophical thought
has been built. This small book, which every candi-
date for government appointment was once required

to know by heart, has incited more than ten thousand commentaries and essays, according to the catalog of the Imperial Library.

Looking at a Chinese edition of the Classic of Changes (see box), one may notice, among the various ideograms, some strange diagrams, all different. These figures are each made up of a stack of six solid or broken lines, which appear as headings for each of the sixty-four "chapters" of the core text. These diagrams exemplify both the unique and the universal aspects of the *I Ching*. In Western languages they are called hexagrams, a term coined by Western translators by combining the two Greek particles *hexa-* (six, as in *hexa*gon) and *-gram* (writing, as in tele*gram*). They are the basic elements of the system underlying the Book of Changes. They are used to represent typical situations, or moments in daily life, devoid of any specificity. These situations have been simplified to their essential characteristics, so there is no longer any trace of the events behind them; the hexagram presents only a combination of their energies, represented as a series of lines.

The *I Ching* is not the only attempt to describe the different facets of the universe with a finite set of symbols. African geomancy is one such system; astrology and tarot cards are others. But none of these other systems attained the level of abstraction of the

A PAGE FROM A CLASSICAL EDITION
OF THE *I CHING*

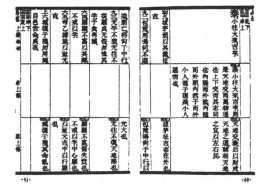

As in all Chinese books published before 1966, the characters are read from top to bottom and from the column at the right toward the left.

On the top right of the page is the drawing of the hexagram (here no. 11). Just to its left, and somewhat larger and bolder than the others, is the character that gives it its name. Just below that is the text of the Judgment. To the left of this column, in the same horizontal section, begin the Line Texts. This upper section contains all the core text of the *I Ching*. The two other sections contain the texts of the official commentaries (the Ten Wings) that are directly related to this hexagram: in the central section is the Commentary on the Judgment; just below is the Great Image with, at its left, the Small Images, the commentaries to each of the Line Texts. The other commentaries are collected at the end of the book.

There are a total of 130 characters on this page, which makes up one of the sixty-four "chapters" of the *I Ching*, which are all arranged in this manner.

I Ching. It has no mythical creatures, such as the horse-man of Mesopotamian astrology; nor does it contain scenes that have no relation to the worldview of non–Judeo-Christian cultures, as the tarot does. The *I Ching* is merely a mathematical representation of two alternate and reciprocal forces: yin and yang.

Because only a binary code is used, the linear figures of the *I Ching* go beyond their purely Chinese origin to attain a universal language. This is not begging the question but simply making an observation that anyone can make, as Gottfried Leibniz once did. You do not need to know Chinese to understand a hexagram, you only need to be able to see the difference between a solid line and a broken line. However, just try to explain to a Chinese who knows nothing of the myth of the centaur, or of Catholic hierarchy, what the sign of Sagittarius means or what arcana the Pope represents. Hexagrams do not need to be translated; it is easy to "read" them directly.

To understand how these figures are used as a system for deciphering the relationships between yin and yang, it is useful to examine how the Chinese language expresses these two ideas. And the best way to know how the Chinese think about a given idea is to look at how they write it.

YIN AND YANG

Unlike words in our language, Chinese characters cannot be capitalized. However, the very pragmatic Chinese mind does not seem to suffer from this graphical impossibility. Therefore, they cannot be written so as to express "key ideas," which exist only as a result of typographical conventions.

Yin and yang do not have their own inherent reality. They do not exist in the same way that this book exists. They are only descriptions, types of movement, alternative indicators of the continual flow of change. This can be seen clearly in the two characters that are used to represent them.

yin 陰   yang 陽

The first thing one notices when looking at these two characters is that the left-hand part of each character is the same: 阝 This sign originally represented the mounds that were built for ritual ceremonies to the gods of the soil. While this is a reminder of the ancient animist religion that was later replaced by the philosophical system of the *I Ching* (see chapter 2), it is also a reminder that yin and yang cannot exist independently. Originally *yin* referred to the northern, dark side of a mountain and *yang* to its southern or sunny side. Heads or tails, we might say; they always make up the two sides of the same reality.

Let us look first at yang. The right side of the character looks very much like the *I* of *I Ching* (see box p. xii). In fact, the only difference between the two is one horizontal line. Whereas *I* evokes the idea of changing weather, or the "ease" with which sunshine and rain may alternate in the sky, yang stresses just one aspect of these changes. The horizontal line clearly separates the sun 日 from the falling rain 勿. This part of the ideogram shows the end of a storm, the moment when the sun has prevailed over the clouds, when it can be seen more and more clearly. Yang is this special moment when the clouds start to dissipate and the sun appears: the air gets warmer and lighter, the sky rises, and the clouds fade away.

The right side of yin is made up of two signs. The first, 今, gives an idea of latent presence, and the second, 云, is the character for cloud(s). This is yang's complementary movement: the rain clouds gather, the sun is hidden, the sky appears lower, and the air becomes darker and colder.

Look at the disparity between the ideas behind these characters and the translations that are usually given for them. Start with the most egregious: yin = feminine, yang = masculine. It is difficult to imagine a more radical reduction of a system whose aim is to represent change. Woman or man: such as we are born, so we remain for our entire life. And it does not help to point out that within each of us is the masculine or feminine counterpart; this separation is too ironclad.

Since the idea of duality is so familiar to us, we are often presented with lists of the opposite qualities of yin and yang, such as

yin	*yang*
dark	light
cold	hot
low	high
night	day
interior	exterior
rest	action

This kind of list may be helpful, but it has one serious disadvantage, and that is the implied existence of the verb "to be" connecting the headings with each of their attributes. This kind of copulative verb, which links a subject and an object, does not exist in Chinese. A Chinese cannot say that yin *is* dark, cold, or low. He or she cannot therefore think that dark, cold, and so forth, are characteristics of yin but only that they are the results that manifest because of its action. Yin is not dark, it is a movement of darkness;

it is not cold but a tendency toward getting cold; it is neither interior nor at rest but rather turning inward and slowing down. The best way to express this particularity might be to use the verb "to become" in place of "to be." Therefore, yang would not *be* light but is *becoming* light; it is not hot, exterior, or action but is becoming hot, becoming external, or becoming action.

Yin and yang are the concerted movements of life and exist only within the dynamics that unite them.

THE YIN/YANG COUPLING

Yin and yang are not static, separate, symmetrical entities. In fact, in order to speak accurately about yin and yang, the two terms must be presented together as one: yin/yang. The essence of yin/yang is neither yin nor yang but the dance created by their union.

Bruce Lee, the "little dragon" of kung fu, knew what dancing was all about. He compared the operation of yin/yang to riding a bicycle.

> As long as you keep trying to separate yin/ yang into two things, you can never hope to realize them. . . . If you want to go somewhere on a bicycle, you cannot push on

both pedals at the same time without remaining still. To move forward, you need
to push on one pedal at the same time as
you let go of the other. The complete
movement is push/release. "Pushing" is
the result of "releasing," and each action
in turn causes the other to happen. . . .

When a practitioner of kung fu has understood the unity of yin/yang, he acts cor-
rectly, whether it is gently or with force: *he
does the right thing at the right time.*[3]

This twentieth-century movie star concluded an article in a martial arts magazine by defining the perfect practitioner of the *I Ching* in a way that even
Confucius would approve of.

The Chinese do not like separating things by de-
grees. The principles behind yin/yang apply to all
levels of thought and action as well as the inner unity
of the Chinese mind. This inseparability of the trivial
and the sublime is something that is specific to the *I
Ching* and that has shocked many Westerners. Those
who see in the *I Ching* a sacred book (some have even
called it the Chinese Bible) refuse to accept its use as
a simple tool for effective decision making, regarding
such use as a sacrilege of its very essence and origin.
Those who use it as a dependable guide for the small
and large decisions of daily life may find it difficult

to accept that such a book has served, for more than two thousand years, as a source of Chinese philosophic thought. The words and ideas of the *I Ching* stand behind almost all Chinese theories of the organization of the universe and the means for human beings to participate in it harmoniously.

The versatility of the yin/yang principle makes it difficult to explain in mere words. But that bothers only us Westerners. The Chinese do not use words to represent ideas, they use abstract ideograms, which combine the rigorous logic of the left brain with the esthetic qualities appreciated by the right brain.

THE DIAGRAM OF THE GREAT REVERSION

For people who do not write with pictures, these abstract ideograms look like simple line drawings. In China, where everything that carries meaning is written as a combination of lines, these drawings represent the summit of ideographism: they are able to express the unseen rhythm of the movements inherent in every living thing.

There is nothing to understand in Chinese symbols. To let them sink in, all you need to do is look at them as if they were animated films. The above abstract symbol is not a geometric form of the kind that

the Greeks appreciated. It is more like a stroboscope.
Yet the movement of infinite reversal that it depicts
has been slowed down and stylized in such a way that
we can only see it as motionless. But it does express
movement. The Chinese name confirms it: The
Drawing of the Great Reversion (*t'ai chi t'u*). It has
also often been called The Drawing of Tao. This is a
classic mistake, which shows how we can get trapped
applying words to Chinese concepts. By its very
essence, the Tao cannot be seen. What is shown in
this drawing is not the Tao but a circular representation of its inner workings.[4]

The two "buds," the white dot in the black part
and the black dot in the white part, show that nothing is ever entirely white or black. But this idea goes
further than what one may see at first; it also shows
that each part contains within itself its counterpart.
It shows that everything is made up of a changing
mixture of yin/yang. What is black will become more

and more white until it is completely so, while the opposite movement occurs for the white part. This movement brings about a change, a complete reversion of the symbol, which in turn initiates the complementary movement, like the pumping and relaxing of a heart. The different stages of the movement can be represented like this:[5]

This is a brilliant example of how the Chinese manage to capture something so profound in just one drawing. The yin/yang perfectly expresses the rhythm of change, the pace of time passing.

The ticking away of time, the passage from one moment to another, these are things we have great difficulty seeing, or even conceiving. Henri Bergson noticed this, as he explained in *The Creative Mind*:

> We think about movement as if it were made up of immobility. . . . Our mind can only remember it as a series of positions: first one point, then another, then another one. If one objects that there must be something between two points, it inserts

new positions between them, and does so indefinitely. It looks away from the transitions. Our mind can only conceive of or express movement according to immobility.

We will see later, when discussing chance (chapter 4), that our mind cannot conceive of chance events without interpreting them according to patterns. This defect is regrettable, because, as Bergson continues,

> We can understand that static concepts may be derived by our mind from a reality in movement; but there is no way to reconstruct the mobility of reality with these static concepts. . . . As a result, our mind is incapable of truly understanding life, which is uninterrupted creation, a continuous flow.

THE ETERNITY OF CHANGE

Duration is one area where the Chinese seem to be experienced. Their civilization may not be the oldest in the world, nor the *I Ching* the "oldest book in the world," as some book-cover blurbs naively claim; the Egyptians and the Sumerians knew how to write at least a thousand years before the Chinese invented ideograms. But today no one uses hieroglyphics or cuneiform writing, while the Chinese are still using the characters invented by their ancestors. Of all existing human civilizations, that of the Chinese has the greatest continuity, and, as of now, there are no indications that they are ready to disappear. It is difficult to imagine that the secret behind such permanence, and its theoretical underpinning, lies in the heart of a book that deals only with change.

Among the sixty-four hexagrams in the *I Ching*, one in particular deals with this subject. It is called Lasting. It is the thirty-second hexagram, and it is right in the middle of the book, as if to highlight the importance of its subject.

What does this key chapter tell us? "The four seasons change continually from one to another. This is how they realize the duration of time" (hexagram 32, Commentary on the Judgment). Its message is very clear: the only thing that is continuous is the perpetual change of all things. Change is the only immutable law in the universe.

This is not just a paradox, such as the Sophists were fond of, or like a Zen koan.[6] It is a clear assertion of what is suggested by the three meanings of the character *i:* the rule of spontaneous change (see box p. xii).

The overall scheme behind the *I Ching* is now becoming clear. The Book of Changes takes up the challenge of what Bergson suggested was impossible. While the symbol of the Great Reversion could only show a global movement, the *I Ching* is an attempt to look at details and achieve the impossible: to show the continuity of the passage of time through a carefully thought-out succession of sixty-four symbolic moments.

The hexagrams themselves are not symbols, they are drawings, X-rays of particular moments within a general evolution. These moments are not static, like those we insert artificially between others to separate two periods of time; rather, they are moments that are happening, in slow motion, at a speed akin to that of the Great Reversion.

Each of these moments makes up a chapter of the *I Ching*. Each of the sixty-four chapters is arranged in the same way (see box p. 3): a linear figure, the hexagram; its name; a general commentary (the Judgment); and six specific commentaries (the Line Texts). The names of the hexagrams sometimes symbolize material objects, but they always evoke particular circumstances or dynamic situations—by describing either those situations or the ideal strategy that one should adopt in such situations. They have names such as Hindering at the Beginning (no. 3) or Learning How to Learn (no. 4) or Making the Most of Waiting (no. 5) (see the appendix). These are moments that we have all met at one turning point or another in our lives, whatever the actual situation surrounding them may be.

The *I Ching* does more than just describe these moments; it animates them. It shows us how they evolve, how each one of them, depending on the circumstances, can change into any of the sixty-three other situations, or even change into itself. This is due to the yin/yang movement that is constantly pulsing within each of the six levels of the hexagrams.

WRITING CHANGE WITH LINES

Hexagrams are made up of two types of lines: continuous (solid), and separated in the middle (broken). These two types of abstract, binary symbols are the result of a long historical process of refinement. They are the graphic equivalents of yin and yang.

yin   yang

But these lines should not be looked at with wide-open Western eyes, wondering why this one is yin and that one yang. It is better to squint a little and see them as the Chinese do.

The closing of a door is called *k'un,* the opening of a door *ch'ien.* One closing and one opening together are called a change. What comes and goes without hindrance is called free penetration. (Great Commentary, Part 1, chapter 11, §4)

Ch'ien and *k'un* are the names of the first two hexagrams of the *I Ching,* the ones that initiate the set of sixty-four changes. They represent the two principles that are set in motion in all of the hexagrams: yin with *k'un,* made up entirely of broken lines, and yang with *ch'ien,* made up entirely of solid lines. The image of a door opening and closing evokes the movement that is constantly taking place within the solid and broken lines.

Yang is a movement of ex-tension.

Yin is a movement of in-tension.

Each yang line should be imagined as being stretched outward, lengthening infinitely, getting so long that it finally splits in the middle and opens like a door. It is the yang movement of lengthening that provokes the change to yin, the split in the middle, by itself. It will then commence a yin movement of contraction inward until the two halves of the line have met. At this moment the other point of return will be reached, the door will be closed, and the flux will reverse again.

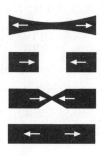

This dynamic tension that exists within each of the six lines of each hexagram is the basis of a refined system of changes and correspondences among all the different figures. We will examine its workings when discussing the individual use of the *I Ching* in chapter 3. But first there is another internal movement to look at, which runs through all the hexagrams and is the result of the second major law of Chinese philosophical thought: the law of analogy.

Reasoning by analogy is as valued in China as it is disparaged in the land of Descartes; but it is looked down upon in the name of the same demand for rigor. One way it manifests in China is as follows: To be accepted as an emblem of a given set, an object must obey the general rule defining the set itself. In *The Library of Babel* Jorge Luis Borges elegantly examines the logical complexity of this problem. In this short story, Borges tells of a librarian who is making a catalog of the library he is responsible for, arranged by subject. He discovers that the catalog he has made of English literature cannot belong to the section on English literature because it, itself, is not a book on English literature but is, rather, a catalog of books on English literature. This is the way that the Chinese perceive the law of analogy. For an emblem to be accepted as the fair representation of a given set, it must obey the general rule defining the set itself.

The figures of the *I Ching* obey the law of analogy. Emblems of the tempo of yin/yang, which animates all living things, they are subjected to the general law of all living things: they "grow" from the ground toward the sky. Hexagrams grow, therefore, from the bottom up: their first line is the bottom one and their last line is at the top. This brings about a vectorization of the figure along the axis of time, a progression within the moment under consideration. Hexagrams are not just frozen images, steps in the pendulum-like movement of yin/yang; they are also endowed with a movement that belongs only to them. They are not sixty-four frozen situations but rather a sort of "mini-opera" that occurs in six episodes: the overture (the first line, on the bottom), the four main acts (the four central lines), and the finale (the upper line). The details of each of these episodes are given by the Line Texts.

Let us look at an example, hexagram 7, which represents a situation of rallying that is characteristic of a "state of war," describing all of the stages of a military campaign. In the first line we see the armies come forth amid a fanfare. A conflict has not been settled in a peaceful manner; the state of war is ahead but the war has not yet started: arms are exhibited in the hope that they will not have to be used. At the last line, the war is over, the mobilization ends with the return of a civilian government, which rewards the victors. Between these two moments, as in all wars, there is nothing but bodies, defeats, pillaging (lines 3, 4, and 5). The *I Ching* shows a war scene in the seventh hexagram, not out of relish, but because the situation of war is a part of life, that of nations as well as that of individuals, and it is important to know how to behave in that type of situation. But beyond the specificity of the episode presented in this figure, it is easy to notice the difference in tone between the four central lines (there is a war being fought) and

THE CORE TEXT OF THE SEVENTH HEXAGRAM

JUDGMENT: Arming. The sign of an opening for a hardened person. No fault.

LINES: *6 at the beginning*. The army goes out to the sound of yang notes. Ponder about the spoils. Obstruction.

9 at the second place. Being at the right place in the army. Opening. No fault. The king confers titles three times.

6 at the third place. It may happen that the army carts away corpses. Obstruction.

6 at the fourth place. The army sets up its camp on the left side [the side of peace]. No fault.

6 at the fifth place. In our farmlands are plundering birds. It is beneficial to stubbornly hold back words. No fault. The eldest son commands the army. The youngest son carts away the corpses. The sign of obstruction.

6 on top. The great leader gives titles. Countries are founded. Feudal clans are established. People of lesser capacity are not retained.

the two external lines (in the first line music is being played, and in the sixth line the country is being re-organized amid the peace and solidarity that have returned).

The two extreme lines of this hexagram are like the black and white seeds in the drawing of the Great Reversion: the first brings the preceding situation to its end (hexagram 6, Resolving the Conflict), and the last prepares for the following situation (hexagram 8, Cohering). This organization of the figures among themselves not only sets each episode within an over-all progression—such that each final line is the em-bryo of the following situation, and each first line the echo of the preceding situation—but also organizes all sixty-four hexagrams in a long series that is not linear but cyclic. Thus the sixty-fourth and final hexa-gram is called Everything Needs to Be Done. It does not represent the ultimate perfection that all things strive for; that role is taken up by the sixty-third hexa-gram, Everything Has Been Done. The final figure of the *I Ching* is really "the one just before the first one." The circle is closed with number 1, Absolute Yang Energy, and the whole series starts over again for a new cycle.

But the Chinese like difficulty. They wondered whether they could give the representation of the en-tire sequence itself the status of an emblem. How

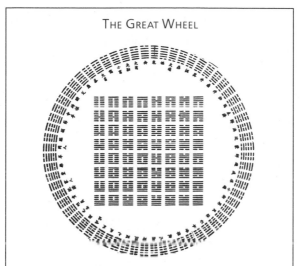

THE GREAT WHEEL

The sixty-four hexagrams arranged in a circle and a square by Master Shao Yung (1011–1077). This diagram is called the arrangement of Fu Hsi and was added to books about the *I Ching* by Chu Hsi (see chapter 2).

would it be possible to show, in graphic form, that the whole set of sixty-four figures obeys the yin/yang rhythm?

The result is the drawing shown. All sixty-four hexagrams are present, and they are present twice because it is showing the Great Reversion. The round part suggests continuity, and the square suggests discontinuity. Heaven is there, turning around the Chinese lands, which are recognized by the multitude of small square fields. It is the entire universe that is being represented here, not in the diversity of the events that make it up, but in the unity of its pulsations.

This picture is the most perfect of all the abstract ideograms found in the *I Ching*. It is not the oldest; it only dates back to the eleventh century of our era, but it is the most accomplished and the most appealing. Its authentic visual harmony leaves you in awe when you realize that each of its elements has gone through its own development, analogous to that which is told by the overall picture, and that each of the six parts of each element also plays the same tune.

This time there is no need to squint to see that hexagrams are like holograms, those frozen images that seem to move, because each of their points contains all of the visual information of the entire image.

How were the Chinese able to create such a device? What logic did they follow? Where did they start and how did they sculpt it and fit in the ten thousand internal cogs of this surprising compass, which is used to find one's way not in space but in time? You will know, dear reader, if you read the chapters that follow, as they say in Chinese novels.

2

From Bronze to Opium
Milestones in the History of the *I Ching*

Legends and myths are necessary to all peoples. They are the explanations of their origins.
For that purpose, the Chinese established, at
the dawn of their civilization, exceptional beings that incarnate the forces that govern the
birth of a great people.

—Claude Larre, *Les Chinois*[1]

THE "GOLDEN LEGEND"
OF THE *I Ching*

The mythological genesis of the "black-haired people" starts out with three "august" figures: Fu Hsi,
the inventor of the *I Ching*; Shen Nung, the Divine
Husbandman; and Huang Ti, the Yellow Emperor.
Five "rulers" just slightly less legendary then took
charge, opening the way for the human dynasties
that would soon merge into authentic history.

Fu Hsi, the most ancient as well as the most important, is the real founding father of Chinese identity. He is credited with the invention of ideographic writing, the institution of rites, the art of counting with knotted cords, the art of cooking, and especially the invention of the *pa kua,* or the "eight trigrams"—the abstract representation of universal energy. His work is an anthology of the best of Chinese civilization, but he also had his own style.

Fu Hsi was not a hero like Prometheus, who stole secrets that the vengeful gods had jealously guarded, in order to better mankind. He was not an inventor either, not one of those knights of progress that were so admired in the nineteenth century. His genius was that he was able to notice and organize signs that appeared suddenly by chance. The Chinese text of this legend does not say that he "invented" the *pa kua* but that he "noticed" them on the back of a turtle that was coming out of the Yellow River, and "organized" them in a way that was beneficial to mankind.

After the period of Fu Hsi's discoveries, a long time went by without any major events. Then came the "incident" between Wen Wang (King Wen) and the tyrant Chou Hsin. This was a banal event during which Chou Hsin, the last ruler of the Shang dynasty, imprisoned one of his vassals whom he had unjustly slandered, King Wen. This event would not have had the honor of being included in Chinese legend if it had not been a major link in the history of the *I Ching*. For, in his cell, King Wen spent his time reflecting on Fu Hsi's trigrams. He came up with the idea of organizing them two by two, thus creating the sixty-four hexagrams. He also gave them each a name and wrote a short paragraph about each one summarizing its meaning: the Judgments. This work gave the king his name: Wen Wang means "the Writer King" or "the Civilizing King" (the same character—*wen*—meaning both writing and civilization). Thanks to King Wen, the *pa kua* grew in importance, now that they were accompanied by written texts. They were no longer just a set of mute symbols.

King Wen's successor, his son the Warring King (Wu Wang), avenged his father. He attacked the tyrant, killed him, and set up the Chou dynasty, which was to rule China for nine centuries. According to the traditional Chinese way of thinking, however, those in the military are not well appreciated. Usually, after having brought back peace, which is the final goal of war, as we have seen in hexagram 7 (p. 21–22), they rapidly leave the stage. As a good legendary model, Wu Wang obeyed this rule. But since, at his death, his son was too young to rule, the regency was entrusted to the boy's uncle, Chou Kung, the wise Duke of Chou.

In order to educate the young heir, Chou Kung perfected the work of King Wen. He wrote short explanations for each of the six lines of the sixty-four hexagrams: the Line Texts.

The entire core text of the *I Ching* was thus established by the great ancestors of the Chou dynasty. Consequently, thirty-two centuries later the Chinese still call the *I Ching* by its more familiar name, the "Chou I," or "the [Book of] Changes (I) of the [court of the] Chou."

It was finally time for Confucius to come into the picture. It is said that he wore out three scrolls of the *I Ching* from his painstaking study of it. It is even reported that when he was fifty years old, he said, "If heaven were to grant me another fifty years of life, I would spend them studying the *I Ching,* and maybe, then, I would make no more mistakes." This attribution is overly generous, just as the legend is that says he wrote all the canonical commentaries, the ones known as the Ten Wings.

Such is the golden legend of the Book of Changes, which ends with Confucius in the fifth century BCE. Not only is the text of the *I Ching* now complete, but it has become a "classic," a *ching*. Because in China, once an important text has been embellished with official commentaries, and in addition, when those commentaries have been attributed to Confucius, it becomes a classic; that is, it is a book that must be studied in class.

This legend, which has been respectfully transmitted from one generation of scholars to the next for more than twenty centuries, still has many believers. This is especially true in the West, where some authors take it at face value and go so far as to give precise dates for Fu Hsi's reign or character traits for King Wen.

Historically, Fu Hsi is a character with as much reality as the Adam of the Bible. As for King Wen and the Duke of Chou, they did exist, but in the way that Achilles or Roland did, carrying out more exploits dead than alive.

For Confucius the story is slightly different. History attests to the facts of his life. Because of this, it is possible to be certain that, like his contemporary Socrates, he wrote nothing himself.

Yet the legend of the *I Ching* is far from nonsense. Like most great historical legends, it tells the truth in a condensed manner, in the way that depth psychology uses the word *condensed*. But unlike other mythological stories that present the genesis of a civilization, the elaboration of a foundation story, or the invention of writing, this story is presented, from beginning to end, as a collective process that involves only human beings: no gods speak, no demiurges act, and no magic happens. No one person invented the *I Ching*. It does not claim to have an author; it was made by itself, like a large patchwork that has accompanied the Chinese people since the origin of their culture, perfecting itself and auto-organizing over the centuries.

THE DISCOVERY OF DIVINATION
(FIRST PART OF THE SHANG DYNASTY, SEVENTEENTH TO FIFTEENTH CENTURY BCE)

> The practice of divination has always been
> widespread in China as well as in all countries
> under Chinese influence, and remains so
> today.—Léon Vandermeersch, "From Turtle to
> Yarrow"[2]

If there is a civilization that is impassioned about divination, it is surely the Chinese. But they are also impassioned about history. After the *I Ching*, the second of the Five Classics is the Classic of History. But in China, history is not seen as a branch of science but as a part of ethics. So it was only at the beginning of this century that the Chinese developed an interest in scientific archeology. Since then, a tremendous wealth of discoveries have been made, which has considerably altered our view of ancient Chinese history and the legends that are related to that period. Above all, these discoveries have shown that the heroes in these legends are not mythological figures born without reason from a wild imagination but personifications of sociological processes. In the light of archeological discoveries, Fu Hsi remains as fictive as Adam, but there is one difference: the period that he represents did exist, about four thousand years ago.

It was during the Bronze Age, in the plain of the Yellow River. In Chinese historical chronology, it was the age of the Shang dynasty. The Shang, who had probably arrived from the wide centrifugal plateaus of central Asia, used the strength of their recently developed bronze weapons to rule over a farming people who had lived in the valley since the Stone Age, if not longer.

The Shang practiced an animist religion. They venerated their late ancestors as well as the spirits of the soil, the rain, the mountains, the thunder, the rivers, and the wind. Fifteen hundred years later these natural realities would appear as symbols for the trigrams, but at that time they were only fickle and cruel deities that had to be placated before any undertaking. Many animal sacrifices were made to them, by cutting the best pieces of meat and placing them on a sacred fire. They would then be allowed to burn down to the bone, because it was thought that the fire had the power to "project" the human offerings up to heaven. It made them "heavenly," that is, such that they would be edible for the spirits. Giving a good meal already seemed the best way for the Chinese to influence the faraway powers on which everything on earth depended. But these practices, which were born out of vague worries, always found themselves up against a more specific apprehension: was the offering acknowledged? How could one be sure that the heavenly spirits gave their consent, without which nothing on earth could last? To answer this question, the Shang priests invented dialectics.

Meticulously observant, as are all Chinese, the Shang priests had noticed that at the end of a ceremony the bones that remained among the ashes were covered with cracks. But these cracks did not exist on the bones in their natural state, nor were they found on the bones of meat prepared for human consumption. Therefore, there must have been some sort of connection with the ceremony itself. And to explain what seems to us the simple result of fire acting on the surface of bone, they went so far as to imagine that the fire was the agent not of one change but two, that it caused a double movement: first a movement *away* from humans toward heaven, from the visible world to the invisible world of the ancestors and the gods, then its complementary movement, a *return,* from above to below, an impulse that, coming from the invisible, materialized at the human level. They could now explain the origin and meaning of these strange cracks. These movements were not the result of chance, nor were they magical or mechanical; they were intentional. They were the return receipt that the gods sent to earth: their verdict. The answers from the gods to the human offerings and questions were there, written in black and bone.

When the Shang priests decided to bestow meaning on these networks of cracks, they became augurs. They could have stopped there, as had their Sumerian and Egyptian counterparts at the same time, only establishing theocratic bodies devoted to the interpretation of divine messages. But they did go further, brilliantly modifying their way of thinking by adding a variable that we tend to overlook: time, the quality of the moment.

In a universe that is ruled by the arbitrary decisions of the gods, it is normal that some sacrifices be accepted and others not. But what surprised the Shang was that *all* of the sacrifices left marks on the bones. There was something that caused the gods to answer the Chinese. Something that ruled both in heaven and on earth. Well, for an agricultural people, what rules the earth is time. A good harvest depends less on the grain that is sown than on the moment that it is planted. So, to the question why one sacrifice to a given god was accepted and another refused, they found the answer: one was made at the right time, and the other at the wrong time. The quality of the moment of the sacrifice was as important as the offering itself, if not even more so. From that point it became logical to look back at the relationship between the sacrifice and the cracks. Indeed, if the examination proved *afterward* that an offering had been accepted, this meant that, on that day, it would be accepted *in principle*. An extraordinary conclusion was developed from this observation: ruled by neither the offering nor the gods, *the effectiveness of a sacrifice existed before it was made.* Since the Chinese are a very pragmatic people, they arrived at the following corollary: Instead of looking for the proof of the acceptance of a sacrifice after it has been made, why not try to be sure before immolating the victims?

This was a very simple idea that completely changed the way the ceremony was carried out. The examination of the cracks, which had until then been an addition to the religious ceremony, was now at the heart of the liturgy. A new ceremonial was developed in which the preparatory augury became the highlight, and the sacrifice a simple concluding rite. The sacrifice was still carried out, but only half-heartedly. The deities, whose answers were inevitable and could be known in advance, lost a lot of their metaphysical prestige. At this moment the Chinese way of thinking developed a characteristic trait. It would be most apparent a thousand years later, when Confucius politely refused to consider transcendental questions. But for the moment, the Chinese did not yet know how to write, and on the other side of the world, the pharaoh Akhenaton was inventing the first type of monotheism.

THE INVENTION OF WRITING
(SECOND PART OF THE SHANG DYNASTY, FIFTEENTH TO TWELFTH CENTURY BCE)

With this possibility of determining the augurs in advance Chinese divination was born. All that was needed then was to "refine the practice while fixing up the theory."[3] To make the cracks more readable, round bones were abandoned for flatter bones, such as scapulae (shoulder blades). Then, instead of placing the bone directly into the fire, a firebrand was used, whose point was applied at just one spot on the bone. It may be that subsequent reflection on this gesture engendered the Chinese idea of applying heat to specific places on the energetic network of the human body, as acupuncturists do when they use moxibustion. It is also possible that the idea of using metal needles for the same purpose came from this divinatory gesture, for the firebrand would soon be replaced by a type of bronze needle, or poker. From makeshift tools to invention, the Shang would finally develop a complete analogical system.

They soon questioned the continued use of animal bones, which were related to the ancient animist sects, because they no longer worried about questioning divine beings but were trying to find their way among the different moments that give rhythm to the universe. In this case, would it not be better to question the universe directly, using as a medium a living form that has an analogical connection with it? Such as the tortoise. The image of a tortoise in China is that of an animal that resembles the universe. Its upper shell is round like heaven, and its lower shell is square like the fields of the earth. And it also possesses the fundamental virtues of the universe: wisdom and longevity.

This change from animal bones to tortoise shells represented much more than just a change of medium. The tortoise shell was used for what it represented, rather than as part of a sacrifice, as with the oracle bones before it. This was the sign that the system of thought had divorced itself from its earliest references. A new manner of thinking was born that was more abstract and was to develop its own hypotheses.

After the divinatory pieces were burned, they were carefully preserved to allow a later comparison between what had been predicted and the actual outcome. But this wise habit ended up posing serious archival problems, not to mention putting a strain on the diviners' memory. They then developed the habit of inscribing mnemonic symbols on the bones and tortoise shells themselves, which summed up their divinatory commentaries. As has often happened in China, this practical experience brought about other major improvements. Almost unbeknownst to them, the Shang diviners had invented Chinese writing.

These signs were ideograms, the first Chinese characters, direct ancestors of the characters used today, and already sharing the same characteristics. Thirty-five hundred years later some of these characters are still in use, unchanged, such as the character for "divination." What other civilization can boast of such an unbroken cultural lineage?

Writing, invented in Sumer to count sacks of wheat, was invented by the Shang to pin down change. By keeping track of their analyses, the Shang diviners were now able to put their prognoses face to face with reality and refine them through trial and error.

But the strangest thing is that less than a century ago, no one in the world knew this! The Chinese themselves had long forgotten it. This connection was not made until the chance discovery in 1899, after a flood of the Yellow River, of the first "library" of Shang divinatory material. Since then, and especially since 1950, hundreds of thousands of these tortoise shells have been found, deciphered, and interpreted. Suddenly Chinese prehistory has been brought back to life. Scientists have been able to reconstruct with certainty the story that we have just reviewed and understand just how authentic the legend of the *I Ching* is.

The figure of Fu Hsi, for example, with his endless list of inventions, now makes sense. He personifies the most remote period of history, when the essential characteristics of Chinese thought were established. But in addition, by associating cooking and rites, writing and divination, the legend highlights the historical process that links them. The finesse of the Chinese text can now be appreciated, where it does not say that Fu Hsi "invented" trigrams but that he "arranged the *signs,* in the shape of *lines,* that were seen on the back of a *tortoise.*" In this perspective, King Wen and the Duke of Chou are also seen in a different light. They become symbols of the period of transcription and organization of all of the divinatory experience accumulated by the Shang.

THE DEVELOPMENT OF THE TEXT
(FIRST PART OF THE CHOU DYNASTY, TWELFTH TO EIGHTH CENTURY BCE)

Writing enlarged the use of divination so much that the diviners found themselves confronted with an unexpected situation: the near extinction of freshwater tortoises in northern China. Since going back to using bones, as before, was inconceivable, they had to find another procedure. For formal divinations they would continue burning tortoise shells. But for "everyday" divinations, they thought of using the supply of tortoise shells they already had in their archives, which was becoming overwhelming.

Theoretically, this would not be a problem, since their divinatory practice had already developed the conception of a global cyclic rhythm of different moments, favorable and unfavorable. It was therefore logical to assume that for each present situation, there should be, somewhere in the archives, at least one tortoise shell with the same type of cracks that would appear if a burning were done for that situation. The important thing was to find the correct one. In other words, how could they make a one-to-one correspondence from an open set of questions to a closed set of answers? The response that the Chinese developed was elegant. They would use chance and tame it with mathematics.

From a practical point of view, this just meant taking a walk in the country to pick forty-nine straight stalks of a plant used for healing wounds that is found along any path: the yarrow. Then the operation is as follows: All of the stalks are held in one hand, and with the thumb, the bunch of stalks is *split in two by chance.* This action is important, because it is an analogy for the firebrand cracking the tortoise shell. Next, the two groups of stalks are counted, using a special procedure, and the remainder is put aside. This operation is done two more times and results in a final remainder that can *only be one of a certain number of mathematically possible values.*

The origin of this method goes back to the shamans, those mediators of heaven and earth, whose rituals were born in Siberian prehistory. The story of

Casting the I Ching
with Yarrow Stalks

A set of fifty yarrow stalks is used to cast the *I Ching*. Before any manipulations are done, one is taken from the bundle and put aside. This represents the ultimate unity. Next, while concentrating on the question, the questioner, who holds the bundle in the left hand, splits it in two parts by the left thumb. One bunch is put down, and from the other, one stalk is taken and put between the ring finger and the little finger of the left hand. The remaining stalks are counted by fours, which represents the four seasons, until there is a remainder of 4, 3, 2, or 1. This remainder is placed between the middle finger and the ring finger. The other bunch that had been put down is then counted by fours, until there is a remainder of 4 or less, and this remainder is placed between the index finger and the middle finger. The stalks that have been placed between the fingers are now assembled and placed to the side. The "discarded" stalks, the ones that have been counted off by fours, are reassembled into one bunch and are split and counted as the first bunch. The second remainder is placed with the first remainder that had been put aside. This operation of splitting and counting and putting aside the remainder is done a third time. After having combined the three remainders, there will be either 13, 17, 21, or 25 yarrow stalks.

These numbers are translated into lines according to the following convention:

    13 = changing yang = 9
    17 = lasting yin   = 8
    21 = lasting yang   = 7
    25 = changing yin   = 6

Through this operation the nature and quality of the first line of the hexagram is obtained.* The operation is repeated five more times to obtain each of the five other lines.

———————————
*See chapter 3, "The Changes of the Lines."

their role in ancient Chinese history has not yet been written, and the classical Chinese, always too proud of themselves, continually repudiated their importance, with the greatest of ingratitude.

The person to whom the school of diviners has attributed this invention—and here, it *is* an invention—was a real person. His name, Wu Hsien—which means "the influential (*hsien*) shaman (*wu*)"—has been found on a number of tortoise shells used for divination. But he has been totally overlooked by the legend of the *I Ching*. However, the core text of the Book of Changes retains the memory of his influence. The thirty-first hexagram (Hsien, Inciting) carries his name, and it is precisely this hexagram that opens the second part of the *I Ching*, just after the first part has been ended by hexagram 30, Overcoming Bedazzlement (also referred to as Fire, whose importance to divination we have already seen). But Wu Hsien really started a new era in the history of the *I Ching*. Not only are the principles he developed still used today when one "casts" the *I Ching* with yarrow stalks (see box p. 42), but by using numbers as *symbols* of classification. To understand the importance of this, we need to go back in time a bit.

The Shang diviners were very meticulous. Not only did they split their questions into two parts (do this?/

not do this?), but especially, they repeated the burning operation a number of times for each part. These series of burnings were usually repeated six times. This is probably one of the reasons that hexagrams are made up of six lines. They also had another practice, which was to differentiate the types of cracks obtained by using symbolic numbers. This procedure would turn out to have important consequences, because it would allow the development of a correlation between the burning of tortoise shells and the counting of yarrow stalks.

In this method, the successive subtractions carried out after the chance splitting of the stalks are designed to yield a series of six standard numbers, which are used to determine the hexagram that answers the question. The method had been the same in the past, with the difference that when the numbers were found they did not lead to a hexagram but to a tortoise shell, whose burning had led to the same order of numbers. All that was necessary was to find the tortoise shell, take it from the shelf where it was stored, read the mantic texts that were engraved on it, and put it back in its place. This procedure was rigorous, analogically rational, and tedious. As the Chinese are pragmatic thinkers, it was not long before they thought to copy the information from the tortoise shells onto a more convenient medium. To do this, they wrote on strips of bamboo that were tied together with bands of leather or silk. What may seem to us a simple change of medium was actually the key to a total change in perspective.

The diviners, now become scribes, were not satisfied with just identically copying the myriad divinatory commentaries that they had at their disposal. They slowly itemized, organized, combined, and arranged all of this empirical data into a system. This is a perfect example of a scientific approach, an exercise that the Chinese enjoy and one in which they are indeed proficient. Using the same method and the same patience, they correlated the open set of symptoms to the closed set of points on the surface of the human body, giving a structure to acupuncture, which, much later, quite naturally used the figures and vocabulary of the *I Ching* to explain its theory. But the diviner-scribes did not foresee this. For the moment, and for the next few centuries, they were busy grouping similar sentences, putting others end to end, and sometimes adding certain new phrases that were called for by the logic that was slowly becoming apparent in the compilation they were creating. But this time it was the bona fide *I Ching* that was being born, because in addition to the text, copied from tortoise shells, the use of yarrow stalks brought with it the theoretical underpinning that had been missing until then: the idea of *change*. Since using the yarrow stalks made divination an operation that cost nothing, the diviners began the practice of obtaining not one but two series of numbers for each question. Then, comparing the two, they would notice what varied from one to the other. This allowed them to draw more precise conclusions about the flow of the way things evolve. As before, they were still concerned with the quality of the moment, but now they were examining its evolution, which allowed much more precise answers. Later, thanks to specific reflection on the symbolic numbers themselves, they would be able to determine the sequence of evolution directly from the series of numbers cast (see chapter 3).

The *I Ching* still bears reminders of this period of its history. The 384 (64 × 6) Line Texts all begin with the placement of one of these symbolic numbers (9 at the beginning, 6 in the second place, etc.; see box p. 22), as if one could hear the voice of a diviner dictating the texts read from a tortoise shell. What remains in the legend of this period of recopying is personified by King Wen, the King of Writing. This explains why his position is somewhat ambiguous. He is the continuer of the past, perfecting the work of Fu Hsi, and at the same time a founder, discovering the hexagrams, creating the Judgments, and even going as far as "inventing" another sequence of the trigrams. This would be perfectly sacrilegious if it had not been the work of a founding father, and it shows that King Wen represents a period of reshaping of original principles. The legendary position of King Wen also tells us why the Line Texts are not attributed to him. Such a meticulous task of arranging, inlaying, and polishing is considered inferior. It could not be attributed to a founding monarch; he would have lost face. This is why the legend credits a second person with that role, one who is not so highly placed—a regent, a manager, an intermediate: Chou Kung, the wise Duke of Chou.

THE CONTRIBUTIONS OF CONFUCIUS
(551–479 BCE)

> I transmit the teachings of the Ancients without creating anything new.—Confucius, *Analects,* chapter 7, §1

Thanks to these diviners turned scribes, the *I Ching* became a book: the first book of the Chinese civilization, which, until 1900, had produced more books alone than all other civilizations put together. This book was not one that the diviners had to carry with them; they knew it by heart. Yet it is this book, written on strips of bamboo, that differentiated them from other shamans, those who analyzed dreams, the flight of birds, or the shapes of faces. One might think that it was the use of the yarrow stalks that set them apart, but their name, in Chinese, makes it clear. Those who use the yarrow are *shih* (*jen*), a character made up from the symbols for shaman and bamboo, which is the same as calling them the "shamans of the book." During the sixth century BCE they traveled throughout China, officiating in all the princely courts, even the most humble, because divination, such a formal and royal practice at the beginning of the Chou dynasty, had become "popular."

Did Confucius frequent shamans? History does not tell us. Legend does not tell us either, but it does say that he frequently consulted the *I Ching,* and that he wore out the silk bands that held together the bamboo strips of his copy three times. This is an edifying story, but it is slightly unrealistic. Confucius did not like shamans, he thought them to be somewhat uncivilized for his taste, but he did like books. He was a very cultivated man and was well versed in the classics. In his *Analects* he quotes from them often. But as far as the *I Ching* is concerned, things are not so clear. One statement from the *I Ching* is recorded in the *Analects;*

Y-king,* or "Book of Changes," sacred book of the Chinese, the first of a series of *kings*. According to the Chinese, the author of this book is Fo-Hi [Fu Hsi], who ruled three thousand years before the Christian era and is considered as the true founder of the Chinese Empire. Confucius gave it its definitive form. The material that makes up the *Y-king* can be divided into three main subjects: metaphysics, physics, and ethics. Confucius must have shortened the metaphysical part, because the *Y-king* hardly mentions this first subject; as for the section on physics, it explains some universal ideas; but here, as in the *Chou-king,* and as in all of Confucius's books, the most extensive part, the largest part, is the part about ethics, and the ethics of the *Y-king* is certainly the ethics of Confucius. Yet one should not think that there is more method or order in a book like the *Chou-king* or in other books containing Confucius's doctrine. Even Father Visdélou had to say, "When I say that this book, the *Y-king,* deals with all subjects, it does not mean, at least for the first two, that it is methodical or ordered; it is only occasionally so and in unconnected bits of the text that are spread out here and there. But what may be considered a fourth subject in this book is that it is a book of fortunes, a book that, since ancient times, has been used for predictions."

Confucius has thus made the Chinese a people without metaphysics, without rational opinions, but who have faith in the most absurd of superstitions. "All ancient Chinese books," says Father Visdélou, "give many examples of these fortunes being used; the canonical book the *Chou-king* refers to it, as do other books, and their stories are filled with other examples. Not only did Confucius approve of these fortunes, but he also taught the art of their use in formal terms, in the canonical Book of Changes, and there is no doubt that this superstition, which is so widespread in this country, is based on the very words of Confucius."

---

*Former transcription for "*I Ching*" in French.

only one, and a statement that has none of the *I Ching*'s typical images. How can this be explained? By looking where this quote shows up in the *I Ching*.

It comes in the third line of hexagram 32, which is at the very center of the *I Ching*: the middle sentence of the middle line of the middle hexagram of the *I Ching*. The appearance of this single quote is even stranger because Confucius's greatest role models were King Wen and the wise Duke of Chou. The only explanation for this discrepancy is that during Confucius's lifetime the "I" was not yet a "Ching." It was just another handbook of divination among so many others, and its structure had not yet been completed. Confucius thought that divination was morally correct, because it allowed one, through the knowledge of the quality of the moment, to "do the right thing at the right time," as Bruce Lee said so well (chapter 1, p. 9). But he could not have been thinking of the *I Ching* that we know because at that time it was far from being finished. In these conditions, the fact that all of the Ten Wings were attributed to the master highlights more the importance that the *I Ching* would have for the future Confucian school than its importance for Confucius himself.

THE GREAT MISUNDERSTANDING

> One moment of yin, one moment of yang, this
> is called the Tao.—*I Ching*, Great Commentary
> Part 1, chapter 5, §1

This sentence, both an old chestnut and a summary of the entire Chinese dialectical system, is a pure product of the *I Ching*. Or rather, of the thoughts the *I Ching* was then inspiring. It is taken from the text made up by the fifth and sixth wings of the canonical commentary. Probably written near the fourth century BCE, this text, also called the Great Commentary, represents the first attempt to reflect systematically on what was until then just a book of oracles. It suddenly raised the *I Ching* to the profoundest and most creative level of philosophy. It is in this text that the concepts of yin and yang appear for the first time in the history of Chinese philosophical thought. The words already existed in the Chinese language, but with their original meanings of yin as the northern, dark side of a mountain, and yang, its southern, or sunny, side. The ideas already existed in the *I Ching*, but in the form of "yielding and solid," or "dark and light." It was the Great Commentary that guaranteed their longevity by giving them the definitive value they now hold, that of symbols representing the alternating movement that animates the universe, the visible traces of the rippling of the *tao*.

But this use of the word should not be misunderstood; there is no idea of Taoism here. In Chinese, the word *tao* is very mundane. It means: "way," "path," or "road," in its literal sense, and "conduct" or "behavior," in its more figurative sense. Almost all schools of Chinese philosophy have used this word in their discourse, the Confucians, like the others, to talk about the suitable attitude of the ruler or the "superior man"[4] that is seen in the *I Ching*, for example. It is through misunderstanding, or exoticism, that many Westerners confine this word to Taoism. In fact, it should be almost the opposite. Because if the followers of Lao-tzu were called the school of Tao (*tao-chia*), it is precisely because they stood out by taking this common word and giving it a special meaning: they used it as the pen name for the indescribable. "Something made from a mixture was there before the Heaven/Earth. We know not its name, it is called *tao*."[5] The confusion has come from the fact that, one thousand years after this sentence was written, in response to Buddhist pressure, Taoist priests organized themselves into a popular religion

and used the symbols of the *I Ching* to their own advantage, the same symbols that still, to this day, can
be seen on their chasubles.

THE INVENTION OF HEXAGRAMS
(FIFTH TO FOURTH CENTURY BCE)

> The virtue of the yarrow is that
>   it is round and heavenly.
> The virtue of the hexagrams
>   is that they are square and wise.
> The meaning of the six levels
>   informs about change.

—*I Ching,* Great Commentary
Part 1, chapter 11, §2

When, in 1937, Mao Tse-tung explained in a famous
article ("On Practice") the dialectical relationships
uniting theory and practice to his troops, he acted
like all Chinese and invented nothing new. He just
rejuvenated an idea that had always been used in
China: that practice refines theory, and theory, in
turn, modifies practice. Their progress can only be
mutual. The first appearance in a commentary to the
I Ching of the ideas of yin and yang, like all "correct
ideas," did not come "out of the blue." It came hand

in hand with an important change in the way the Book of Changes was used in practice.

We have seen how the different types of cracks on the tortoise shells were annotated with numerical symbols that allowed, at a later date, the substitution of yarrow stalks for the burning procedure. It must be understood then that each chapter of the *I Ching*, at the time the Great Commentary was written, was headed by a column of six numbers that both represented and summed up, first, a succession of burnings, then later, a series of splits in the bundle of yarrow stalks.

How did it come about that these columns of numbers were replaced by stacks of lines? This is not clear, since no documents from this period have been discovered. Nevertheless, researchers agree that the philosophical leap, which is evident from the appearance of the yin/yang couple, must be related to the creation of symbols more abstract than numbers to illustrate the sixty-four typical situations of the *I Ching*. This modification is much less formal than it seems. To the Chinese it completely changed the graphical status of these "headers." Only for Westerners, who write with letters, does one symbol equal another. In China the constraints of ideographic writing give each character its own reality. By becoming sets of lines that a brush has drawn in a precise order, the series of numbers of the *I Ching* become more than hexagrams; they transform into ideograms. From then on, for the Chinese, they are more than just simple instants that help them find their way in the diversity of moments, especially because these figures have a quality that is unique compared with the other ideograms used in Chinese writing: they do not have any pictorial basis. That is why, in the previous chapter, I have called them abstract ideograms. They do not represent anything visible, just the time that passes. One can now see how such figures could have become the very symbols of change, of which yin and yang became the mechanisms.

The figures of the *I Ching* having reached this stage, their appeal to Chinese thinkers would continually increase. They ended up becoming more important than the divinatory text itself—a strange reversal of roles that recalls the change that took place between the sacrifice and the examination of the cracks. But this is also the root of an unshakable misunderstanding that many Westerners have focused on, infinitely repeating the peremptory judgment of the great French sinologist, Marcel Granet: "Sixty-four drawings, the hexagrams alone, make up the real text of the *I Ching,* the rest is just commentary, amplifications, legends."[6]

The Canonization of the Text
(Han dynasty, 206 bce to 221 ce)

As a result of technical inventions that drastically changed productive and military relationships, the Chou dynasty ended with two centuries of internecine wars, in a period known as the Warring States. Because of its violence and its creativity, this period is similar to the Renaissance in Europe in the sixteenth century. An old order was crumbling while, from the everyday tumult, there emerged "one hundred flowers and one hundred schools," that is, new ways to organize and understand the world. This period ended in 221 ce, with the creation of the Chinese Empire by Ch'in Shih Huang Ti, the ruler of one of the many existing kingdoms, who systematically conquered the others.

Ch'in Shih Huang Ti was an implacable autocrat. The spectral army of clay soldiers that stands guard over his tomb in Sian is proof of this. It was not healthy to disagree with him. Yet the scholars of his period who claimed filiation with the teachings of Confucius did just that. In 213, in order to cease any discussion about his legitimacy as emperor, Ch'in Shih Huang Ti gave the terrible order to burn all books and to bury alive any scholar who resisted this order. Works of ethics, politics, and history were especially hunted down by this auto-da-fé, which, however, spared all books on agriculture, medicine, and divination. Because of this, the *I Ching* was saved from the flames, but it did not make it through completely unscathed.

Burning these books also had a practical reason: to unify writing for the characters used in the land of Ch'in by prohibiting the innumerable versions of characters that had proliferated in the different kingdoms. Each kingdom had developed its own style, and these different styles were becoming unintelligible to people from other regions. To achieve this unification it was necessary that *all* books be burned, which was effectively done for all authorized books after they had been copied in the officially accepted characters. However, not all copies of forbidden books were destroyed, because there were enough courageous scholars to hide them, even at the risk of their lives. Their courage enabled them, once the storm had passed, to restore the original texts with certainty. Since the *I Ching* was authorized, as a practical manual, it did not have this luck. Even worse, the absence of any original ancient text would open the door to any future additions. And the Han scholars did just that.

The Chinese like to call themselves the sons of the

Han, because this dynasty, which saw the development of their cultural patrimony, is one they hold dear. To the political and economic unification that was accomplished by Ch'in Shih Huang Ti, the Han added the moral and ideological unification that would hold China together for two thousand years. For the most part, this unification was the work of Confucian scholars who provided the intellectual framework of their dynasty, as the Han had requested. With this end in mind, they started by creating Confucianism, that is, the compilation, organization, and standardization of all the texts attributed to the master or to his great continuators. The version of the *I Ching* that we know today dates from this period, as does its consecration as the first of the Five Classics.

This kind of consecration could not be accomplished without a little bit of touching up. For the commentaries that existed already, it was enough to add the all-purpose formula "The Master said . . ." here and there, for the attribution to Confucius to be accepted as plausible. But the core text posed a different kind of problem for the scholars. The appearance of a hexagram during a divination, and the appropriateness of its text to the situation, had been established and grounded in long experience. But what was still missing was the internal organization of the entire system, an internal logic that would explain both its workings and its history.

THE BIRTH OF TRIGRAMS
(HAN PERIOD)

The question of organization had not troubled the diviners. To find a given hexagram they would just go through the text in their mind, like a computer would. But it seemed essential to Confucian scholars. They wanted to find the deep structure that was at work within the *I Ching* in order to apply it to the overall organization of society. Take a set of empirical data and transform it into a coherent system; that was the Chinese leitmotiv. The final perfection they would achieve in organizing the *I Ching* almost made them forget that, before anything else, they needed to resolve the problem of the text of the *I Ching* itself. It is true that this oversight was brought on by the destruction of all copies of the text that existed before the burning of the books. Confucians do not like to show their rough drafts; it is a question of "face." This entire period, during which the *I Ching* was searching for its own structure, was completely hidden until archeologists discovered evidence such as the Ma Wang Tui manuscript.

According to the "golden legend," the eight trigrams are the basis for the *I Ching* through the grace of Fu Hsi, and the hexagrams thanks to Wen Wang. But in the Ma Wang Tui manuscript, although the hexagrams are organized graphically according to series of three lines, the trigrams themselves are absent. Neither their names nor their common attributes are seen. One must conclude that the "idea" of the trigram is subsequent to the period that this manuscript was buried. It is likely that the Confucian scholars of the Han period, by dint of their analysis of the core text, brought forth these ideas. This "invention," an invention in the same sense that Newton invented gravity, gave them the key to clearing up the apparent incoherence of the divinatory texts, which, while not being without rhyme, were certainly without reason.

Certain sentences appeared often, such as "It is advantageous to cross the great river." Nothing could seem to justify the presence of this phrase in a given hexagram but not in another. Nothing until it was noticed that in most of the cases where it appeared, there was also a figure containing a certain sequence of three lines. From that moment on, the idea of *isolating* that series of lines and considering it equal to the hexagrams, significant by itself, was developed. Using that as a starting point, and looking backward at its relationship to the core text, the image of water and the symbol of danger were naturally given to it, since crossing a river in China is always considered dangerous. Gradually, meanings were defined for the eight possible series of three lines, the trigrams.

It is interesting to note that by using this inversion

of relationship between the ancient text and the linear figures generated by its use, the Han scholars were repeating, unawares, the same change in perspective developed by their ancestors, the Shang diviners. This advancement was certainly at a higher level of abstraction but, in accordance with Chinese constancy, still carried out on symbols in the shape of lines.

Now the magical, shamanic aspect of the divinatory text, so disliked by the Confucians, was tamed. Divination became totally serious, no longer based only on the efficacy of tradition but also on the rationality of analysis.

With the discovery of trigrams, the *I Ching* became not only logical but also pedagogical, which was an essential virtue in the eyes of the Confucians. Since each trigram could correspond to a type of attitude, they could look at a hexagram as a combination of trigrams and infer the pair of attitudes that would be exactly appropriate to the situation. A set of sixty-four typical behaviors would therefore be written and added to the canonical commentaries under the name of the Images. In current translations, these commentaries (the third and fourth wings) are presented between the Judgment and the Line Texts of each hexagram. Their normalized structure and typically Confucian vocabulary clash with the informal vitality of the more ancient texts. The artificial nature of this addition is generally unnoticed and it unconsciously reinforces our belief in the venerability of the trigrams. The exaggerated use that the Han and their followers have made of them also contributed to this belief. Through the possibility of reducing the necessary diversity of sixty-four situations to only eight basic building blocks, these trigrams do hold a certain fascination; by "distilling" the *I Ching,* they seem to approach the very essence of change. And by laying these symbols of symbols out in a compasslike shape, one can see a perfect blueprint of the deep structure/movement that runs the universe.

But in this case, a question must be asked. How is it that a discovery of this importance, which would have overjoyed any philosopher in ancient Greece, was never attributed to Confucius? Probably because it greatly embarrassed the scholars that made it. It must be said that in China an innovator is seen initially as a rebel, because he is upsetting the established order. By inventing trigrams and inserting them as the original basis for the *I Ching,* the Confucians were upsetting its history. They needed to give them ancestors that were as important as they were. This is why they created the legend of their invention and gave credit to Fu Hsi for having discovered them. And to make sure that this discovery would merge seamlessly into legend, the Han scholars, as opposed to Western translators, did not give a different name to these new figures. In Chinese, hexagrams and trigrams are called the same thing, *kua,* divinatory figures. Only the addition of a number (eight or sixty-four) enables one to know which ones are being discussed.

Since the invention of trigrams was attributed to Fu Hsi, it took its rightful place in an honorable past and became part of a genesis so logical that, even two thousand years later, it seems perfectly natural to most believers of marvels.

Finally, for Confucians, the choice of Fu Hsi presented a certain number of advantages. It allowed them to eliminate from the past of the *I Ching* any traces of influence from shamans, and it gave the *I*

Ching seniority over all Taoist texts (the Marquis of Tai also had a copy of the *Tao-te Ching* with him). These texts had been placed under the patronage of the Yellow Emperor, Huang Ti, the third of the first "august" rulers, who was, therefore, subsequent to Fu Hsi. Just like their master, a good Confucian could not resist kicking a real Taoist.

Now that, at the end of the Han period, the *I Ching* was established in history, its figures organized, with a commentary by the master himself, nothing else was needed except an agreement on the order of the chapters. It would take a rare genius to accomplish that task.

Wang Pi, the Rimbaud of Chinese Philosophy (third century ce)

At the end of the Han period the *I Ching* looked more or less as it does today—with one exception: the sixty-four hexagrams were organized incoherently. Let it be clear: this does not mean that in an edition from that period the hexagrams were in a random order, but that at the time a number of orders were used; the order that we know in current editions had not yet been officialized. Arranging, classifying, organizing: that is the eternal obsession of the Chinese. Whether it is for plants, acupuncture points, or characters, the problem is always the same: how can one organize the information taken from reality in a way that is both rational and efficient? Think, for a moment, how difficult it is to make a simple dictionary for a language that has no alphabet, which therefore cannot be organized in any alphabetical order.

Since the Warring States period the question of the order of the hexagrams had been explored, and during the Han period many solutions were proposed. This question was not finally resolved until the seventh century, when K'ung Yin T'a had the text of the *I Ching* engraved on stone slabs, which can still be seen at the museum in Sian. The Imperial edition that was chosen for this engraving carried the explicit name of "Orthodox Interpretation of the (Book of) Changes of the Chou" (Chou I Chenge I).

Why, among all of the solutions suggested by Han scholars, did old K'ung Yin T'a choose to officialize an order for the hexagrams that had already been proposed in the second century BCE by Fei Chih, but which was not the oldest order, as has been seen with the Ma Wang Tui manuscript? Because this order was recommended by an astonishing young man, Wang Pi.

Wang Pi was exceptionally gifted. As the sinologist

M. I. Bergeron has said, "He crossed Chinese history like a meteor, both as a revolutionary and with a thirst for the waters of the sources."[7] Born in 226, he died at the age of twenty-four. But in his short life he had the time to write commentaries on the *Tao-te Ching*, the *I Ching*, and the *Analects* of Confucius, which, seventeen centuries later, still remain remarkably astute.

> To the existential ethics [of Confucius] he gives a mystical foundation, and to the mysticism [of Lao-tzu] he gives the existential basis to continue it. He reconciles contraries according to a logic not of exclusion but of inclusion, where the very idea of opposition becomes a synonym of participation,

says M. I. Bergeron, who continues:

> The dialectics of Wang Pi goes beyond the rivalries of any given school of thought to reach a much wider level that transcends them and integrates them in a universal dynamism.[8]

Wang Pi felt that the order established by Fei Chih was the most satisfying; it was based on the idea of following each hexagram with one obtained by turning it upside down (except in the cases where the figure was symmetrical, where its line-by-line opposite was taken). This organization, Wang Pi felt, gave the best example of the idea of change through the inversion of yin/yang. Four centuries later, the imperial commission presided over by K'ung Yin T'a followed this young man's advice and consecrated the sequence of hexagrams that we are familiar with, attributing it to King Wen. The *I Ching* had found its now traditional form. All that remained, before meeting the West, was for it to get dressed up in new clothes that would be embroidered by the Neo-Confucians.

NEO-CONFUCIANISM
(SUNG DYNASTY, 960–1279)

Buddhism became so important at the end of the T'ang dynasty that the empire almost literally imploded. Rich believers left their land to monasteries, and since they were tax-exempt, state revenues started declining. This decline was so strong that, in spite of their splendor, the T'ang fell at the first serious attack by barbarians.

A new period of division ensued until the Sung

were able to reconquer the entire country. Once this was achieved, the Sung found themselves up against the same problem that the Han had faced: how to unify the territory on a solid ideological foundation? They used the same tactics as the Han, calling in Confucian scholars, who brought in the *I Ching* to assist them. But it was not as simple as it had been before. They now had to take into account the new ideas that Buddhism had brought to the Chinese. They therefore needed to start by renewing Confucianism; that is, by reinterpreting the classics.

The idea of individual liberation through the wheel of karma, for example, would be reformulated in terms of consonant spontaneity with the yin/yang movement of the universe; and the idea of the illumination of the heart was seen as an inner search for the authentic self, having direct hold on the Tao (the influence of the Taoists had to be taken into account also). Out of this came a sort of evolutionist naturalism, both rational and syncretistic, which would be called, in English, neo-Confucianism, and in Chinese, logic of reality or learning of the Tao. This movement may be compared to that which would occupy the European theologians two centuries later when they attempted to harmonize their Greco-Roman heritage with the doctrines of Christian theology. The major difference between the two was that

THE BUDDHIST INTERLUDE
(T'ANG DYNASTY: 618–907)

After the Han dynasty, the empire broke up. The barbarians from the northwest settled in. They spread a strange religion, Buddhism, which would considerably modify Chinese intellectual history. Coming from India via Afghanistan, where it crossed paths with Greek art, Buddhism entered China in the first century by the Silk Road. It did not expand until around the fifth century, when it became the official state religion of the T'ang.

The T'ang dynasty was one of the high points of Chinese civilization, as far as art and science were concerned, and a period of decline for the *I Ching*. Faced with the power of the Buddhist clergy, the Taoists organized themselves in a sort of magical-alchemical brotherhood, which wore the symbols of the *I Ching* on their robes and made them into popular talismans for which the peasants paid dearly.

As for the Confucians, who had been removed from their public offices, they would spend their undesired spare time writing the most beautiful poetry in Chinese history, but they ignored the *I Ching* entirely. The main catalog of the Imperial Library lists only about ten authors, at the section about the *I Ching*, for this period of three centuries. The revival would come with the Sung—more than a hundred authors in less than two centuries: this was the neo-Confucian school that would influence Chinese scholars, and especially Western translators, up until the present.

in China they would still use the venerable *I Ching* as the foundation.

But it was no longer a question, as it had been under the Han, of touching up a divination manual to make a classic. The *I Ching*, its text, and its history could no longer be changed. It was necessary to find something new and hope that, this being China, it would look as old as possible. The Sung took a close look at the hexagrams and examined their numbers. Numbers had become very important in this period, since their logic fit well with the rationalist and abstract necessities of neo-Confucianist ideology. Algebra, for example, took on an importance that the West would not appreciate until after the Renaissance.

It was Master Shao Yung (1011–1077), a famous numerologist and Taoist precursor of neo-Confucianism, who can be credited with bringing to the *I Ching* what it was still lacking: a formal method for both mathematically organizing the figures and logically explaining how they were generated.

Shao Yung took as a starting point a passage from the Great Commentary, where it says, "The Book of Changes expresses the *t'ai chi*. This generates the two principles. The two principles generate the four images. The four images generate the *pa kua* (eight figures)."

The expression *t'ai chi* is difficult to translate into English. *T'ai* gives an idea of extreme greatness, and *chi* of climax. Within a dialectical philosophy, any climax creates a reversal and changes itself into its opposite. We would be close to that idea then if we translated it as "great reversion," as we did in the previous chapter (p. 11). The genius of Shao Yung lies in his application of this passage of text directly to the lines of the *I Ching*. For him the great reversion can only be the movement of Tao. Invisible by its very nature, it can only materialize at the human level through the "two principles." But the two principles, he said, are not only yin and yang; they are also the two types of lines in the *I Ching*. This is the basis for a complete system. The "four images" are no longer the four seasons (as the rest of the text suggests); they become a theoretical division of yin/yang applied to each of the two principles. These are represented by four types of two-line figures, whose direction goes from bottom to top, which could be called bigrams, but which are *kua* in Chinese, like all the other such figures. Considering that the change affects first the bottom line, then the top line, we can look at the four figures in the following order of evolution: the culminating yin ☷ *(t'ai yin)*, then the budding yang ☳ *(shao yang)*, the culminating yang ☰ *(t'ai yang)*, and finally the budding yin ▬▬ ▬▬ *(shao yin)*. The next level of organization, the *pa kua,* is, of course, the trigrams. But instead of their being organized in a cycle, like on a compass as the Han had, they are now organized in a linear sequence from one to eight, from *ch'ien* ▬▬▬▬▬, heaven, to *k'un,* ▬▬ ▬▬, earth. Next, by again adding an additional line on top, the system continues on its own: the eight trigrams generate sixteen "quadrigrams," which then develop into thirty-two "pentagrams," which finally become the sixty-four hexagrams. Ordered from one to sixty-four, still going from heaven to earth, they appear this time in a strictly combinatory order, that is, entirely independent of their divinatory meanings.

Shao Yung's work was a resounding success in China. His astonishing synthesis fit well in the present atmosphere. The Confucians appreciated his starting from a classical text, as well as the rigorous internal logic of his proof. As for the Taoists, they appreciated the use of *"t'ai chi"* as a pseudonym for what they called Tao. The Buddhists also appreciated the lack of precision of this primordial *t'ai chi,* which allowed them to see the impermanence of the universe in action.

The creation of the world is a problem that has never intrigued the Chinese, but it has, of course, always interested Indo-Europeans. When the first Eu-

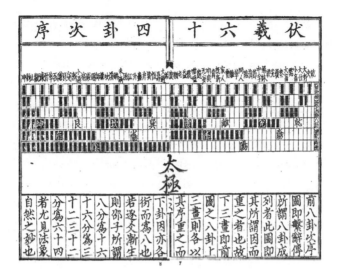

ropean missionaries discovered the *I Ching,* the concepts that had been developed by Shao Yung appealed to them. They saw the *t'ai chi* as a sort of avatar of the original energy of their religion, a primitive form of the Judeo-Christian revelation. This can be seen in the translations that are generally used for the term *t'ai chi:* "Supreme Ultimate" or even "Great Primal Beginning."[9] This misunderstanding, which still continues, would be sealed one hundred years later when the name *t'ai chi* was given to the image of the Great Reversal, as we have seen in chapter 1. It confirms its extraordinary power of syncretism. It must be said that this image is appealing; its binary logic conforms to our normal way of thinking, and it allows us, as Alain Daniélou said so poignantly, to "take from the great traditions only that which does not interfere with our ideas too much."[10]

The order of the hexagrams as often seen on the covers of translations of the *I Ching* in European languages is a different one, which is also the work of Shao Yung, and derived from the previous one, even though he is never credited with its creation. It is even more abstract, and it has no Chinese characters on it; gazing at it, it is easy to imagine that one is looking at the very work "of Fu Hsi who ruled over China five thousand years ago," as Leibniz said. This is the image that is shown in the preceding chapter (see box p. 24).

The movement started by Shao Yung would open the door to a total reconstruction of the interpretation of the *I Ching*. This would be seen in the work of the Ch'eng brothers and especially in the work of the philosopher Chu Hsi, of whom R. Grousset said, "He can be considered as . . . the Thomas Aquinas of China." Chu Hsi (1130–1200) perfected the work of synthesis that was occurring during his period by writing reinterpretations of all of the Confucian classics, and especially two books devoted to the *I Ching*: *Chou I Ch'i Meng* (The *Chou I* for Beginners) and *Chou I Pen I* (The Basic Meaning of the *I Ching*).

These two books are important to examine, not so much for the influence they have had in China for the past seven centuries as for their later influence in the rest of the world. This influence stems from one idea and one detail.

The idea concerns a drawing that may seem almost trivial to us, since we see so many variations on it in advertisements and on T-shirts. It is generally called the yin/yang [or Great Reversal] drawing. Neither is this image specifically Chinese (it can be seen on Gothic cathedrals) nor does it belong specifically to the Sung period (these graphical elements already existed during the Han period), but its fame is due to Chu Hsi. One day, while he was reflecting on Shao Yung's initial *t'ai chi*, he thought that this drawing would illustrate it well. He decided to make it the keystone of the *I Ching* by calling it the diagram of *t'ai chi*.

The detail in question was strictly practical: the Sung invented the printing press. Therefore, *all* printed books date from that period or later. Since Chu Hsi had decided to include the Great Reversal drawing and the Great Wheel of Shao Yung in his treatises on the *I Ching*, all subsequent Chinese books on the subject also contain these drawings on their pages. This unconsciously reinforces our impression that they have always been a part of the *I Ching*, since the oldest times.

These drawings are also found in every Western translation of the Book of Changes, which is doubly misleading, since these fine new clothes that were embroidered by the Sung have absolutely no utility for the individual user of the *I Ching*. The paradox is that neither Chu Hsi nor the neo-Confucians of the Sung period viewed divination unfavorably; quite the contrary. They had greatly contributed to its popularization by inventing the coin method of casting the *I Ching*, which is much faster and easier than using yarrow stalks. One can appreciate the elegance of calling this the King Wen method *(wen wang k'o)* of consulting the *I Ching*. Since it was new, it naturally had to be placed under the patronage of a great ancestor. But attributing it to Wen Wang rather than to Fu Hsi was a subtle way of saying that although it was of a certain age, it was still created after the period in which the *I Ching* was first developed.

CONTACT WITH THE WEST
(CH'ING DYNASTY, 1644–1911)

After the Sung dynasty, Chinese history changed drastically. For the first time in its history the country was occupied by foreigners: the Mongols. During this period (Yüan dynasty, 1277–1367) and the period of restoration that followed (Ming dynasty, 1368–

THE COIN METHOD OF
CASTING THE I CHING

To cast the *I Ching* with coins, three similar coins are used. There is absolutely no obligation to use ancient Chinese coins; any coins will do, as long as one can make out which side is heads and which is tails. The following equivalents are used:

tails = yin   heads = yang

While concentrating on the question, you cast the three coins at the same time and observe which sides are up. There are two possibilities:

If all three coins are showing the same side, the line is changing (yang if there are three heads, yin if there are three tails).

If two coins are showing one side, and one the other, the line is lasting, or unchanging, and it is the side of the coin that is different that determines whether the line is yin or yang (in other words, two yins and one yang would be a lasting yang line).

After the first line is obtained in this way, the operation is repeated five times, for the other five lines of the hexagram.

1644), little of consequence occurred concerning the *I Ching*. Then it was the turn of the Manchus to occupy the empire (Ch'ing dynasty) until it became a republic in 1911. For our purposes, this time marks the beginning of significant exchange between China and Europe. The French king Louis XIV, in particular, sent to Beijing a number of Jesuit missionaries, which were chosen for their high level of cultural and scientific knowledge. They learned the language, customs, and mores of the country and became true scholars. They gave us the first translations (in Latin) of the Confucian classics. One of them, Father J. Bouvet, even sent a copy of Shao Yung's Great Wheel to Leibniz. Fooled by the attribution of this diagram to Fu Hsi, as were many others, the philosopher from Leipzig saw in the image an ancient ancestor of the mathematical system that he had just invented. This episode, which is in reality of little importance, has often been cited as the first contact between the *I Ching* and the Western world; it only marks the beginning of a misunderstanding that has continued up to the present.

In the nineteenth century, the relationship between China and the West would finally become more colonial. The English opened trade routes with gunboats, and started the Opium War. The missionaries that poured into China following the merchants became particularly interested in the *I Ching,* not in order to enrich themselves, of course, but to fight against it, as well as all the other native superstitions. This attitude permeates the first translations of the *I Ching* into Western languages.

A brief mention should be made of the best-known of these translations, the one made by Richard Wilhelm, published in Germany in 1924. The author, although a protestant missionary, boasted of having never baptized any Chinese. He did, however, put all his faith into the translation of what he considered to be a work of pure wisdom. Fifty years later, hippies and

New Agers made it a best-seller, and his version, as well as the others that are "adapted" from his translation, is now the bible for amateur diviners. But it is not a book of divination. Since sinologists have never done anything to clear up this misunderstanding, it is time that we examine what actually happens when the *I Ching* is used in an individual perspective.

3

Yarrow Stalks, Coins, and Tea Leaves
Using the *I Ching*

> When at rest, the *chün tzu* studies the symbols and reflects on the Commentaries. When in action, he studies the changes and reflects on the oracles.
>
> —*I Ching*, Great Commentary
> Part 1, chapter 2, §6

DIVINATION?

Before designing the Statue of Liberty, the French sculptor Frédéric-Auguste Bartholdi had worked on another project for a giant statue that was to be placed overlooking the Suez Canal, at its Oriental end. This statue was to represent Western science bringing enlightenment to the peoples of the Levant. The canal's financial affairs prevented this project from being carried out, and the artist's design now stands in New York Harbor.

Bartholdi's original idea sums up the way the West perceived Oriental civilizations. One can only imagine how the *I Ching* was perceived by those who took the trouble to translate it in order to better fight its ideas, which seemed to be nothing more than native superstition and prelogical mumbo-jumbo.

Today the *I Ching* is looked at somewhat differently. Many people are becoming interested in it for what it is: one of mankind's great texts; and many others for what it is not: a work of divination.

Over the past few decades the number of copies of the *I Ching* sold in Western languages can be counted in the millions. If the work of Carl Jung has helped contribute to its recognition, it was more the hippies of the sixties that made it a best-seller. But these people were not particularly interested in sinology. What attracted them to the *I Ching* was its practical applications in daily life. Unawares, they helped carry on the lineage, which extends back to ancient China, for which theory without practice is like "a plant without roots, drifting with the currents." Unfortunately, since they tended to mix the *I Ching* with any kind of esoteric system they could find, the interest they brought to it only served to reinforce the old colonial prejudice that saw in it only an exotic variation of divinatory superstitions that modern reason could reject without second thoughts.

Divination is a word that was created from the root *divine,* which means "to create a link with the divine through oracles or soothsaying." Even though I have already used the word *divination,* it is not really appropriate for the *I Ching.* But I have done so simply because there is no satisfactory word in English to describe what the *I Ching* actually does. Not only does its history show that it is not used to "foretell future events or discover hidden knowledge by occult or supernatural means,"[1] but its practical use shows that such is not its goal.

Keeping the question of chance and its manifestations for the next chapter, we will now examine the outlook that one can develop through using the *I Ching.*

Unlike any kind of fortune-telling, prophecy, or magic, the *I Ching* does not tell the future, it can only analyze the present. Its use does not allow one to make forecasts, only diagnoses. If there were a comparison possible with a Western equivalent, it would not be to the crystal ball but to a chess-playing computer program that analyzes the current situation in order to choose one of a number of options. In the Chinese domain, it is the equivalent of the acupuncturist who takes the patient's pulse; a similar action is taken when a hexagram is cast. These are both means of determining information about the organization of energy in terms of yin/yang for a given person at a given moment. The acupuncturist uses the pulse to determine which treatment is appropriate not only to the patient but also to the current season. In the same way, the user of the *I Ching* interprets this information to adopt the attitude that harmonizes with the current moment of a given situation, according to his or her involvement in that situation. In short, what Fu Hsi invented was a technique to help in decision making.

The only problem is that, even presented in this manner, its most common method of utilization, that of throwing coins (see box p. 77), gives the *I Ching* "bad press." This practice gives one the unconscious impression of making decisions just by tossing a coin, which, with the exception of the beginning of the Super Bowl, is generally not taken seriously. One may wonder why, since making a decision is, by its very nature, an irrational action, especially when the decision has been the object of long reflection. Accumulating as much information as possible, reflecting on the pros and cons: all this is not actually making a choice but preparing for it. Deciding is judging. The first thing one does is to decide to *stop* weighing the reasons for or against something. Yet our mind has no reason to stop thinking about a decision, as many eternally indecisive people know. You have to make up your mind; you always choose by "intuition," and a decision, as equitable as it may be, is only efficient if it is in concert with the moment. Stockbrokers know this as well as farmers. This is where the *I Ching* comes in: the appropriateness of the moment has always been its concern, since its beginnings. But how can something so ancient, so distant, still function in our modern world? All you need to do to find out is use it.

THE QUESTION OF THE QUESTION

> The good general has already won the battle
> before starting it. The bad general fights in
> hope of winning.
>
> —Sun-tzu, *The Art of War* (third century BCE)

You do not ask the *I Ching* what tomorrow's weather will be, or which football team will win on Sunday. Not because it would be a lack of respect for it (how can you lack respect for a book?) but because it would be illogical. This type of question, like all requests for information about the future, is for fortune-tellers or prophets.

The *I Ching* deals with the present. But this present

is neither frozen nor external, it is the momentary state of a situation that exists as long as we are involved with it. For, ultimately, what the *I Ching* analyzes is ourselves. This is how it can be compared to an acupuncturist's taking of our pulse. This analysis is fundamentally one of "energies" and can have meaning only within a perspective of action. This is why the *I Ching* can be compared to a chess-playing program. A game is going on, there is a goal to achieve, according to the layout of the pieces, and the program decides what the best way is to reach that goal, what is the most efficient strategy. The *I Ching* is not a technique for introspection but an incitement to action. The Chinese would readily present it as a handbook for strategy.

This point of view radically changes the way we use it. The best questions to ask of the *I Ching* are those with a verb of action whose subject is the person asking the question. Asking the *I Ching* if a project will be a success would be simple divination. For this type of question, tea leaves are more efficient. Ask the *I Ching,* however, what is the best way to make the project a success. It will then answer you by proposing the most appropriate strategy, according to the moment, to yourself, and to the project in question.

To understand how this works, imagine the following parable: We are travelers crossing the Land of Life, and the *I Ching* is an old farmer who has lived there all his life. If we ask him a question such as "Will I go to the capital one day?" what would you expect him to answer? He knows neither you nor the future. But he knows his country. He has lived there so long that he knows all its rhythms and, above all, the signs that precede any change. That is why he will be able to help us, as long as we ask him a question that addresses a precise action, and do not ask for general information about the future. If you ask this old farmer, "How do I get to the capital?" then the old Chinese man, like his ancestor Fu Hsi, would first look up at the sky, thinking about the quality of the moment. The clouds gathering in the western sky indicate that there is a good chance of rain. Next he will look at the way you fit into the moment, what physical and moral resources you have, what "energetic equipment" you have, and how it fits your goal. Do you have food? Do you have good shoes, or maybe boots? Finally, combining the information from these two types of observations, he will show you the best path to follow. "Three days' walk along the bank of the river, five by the pass. It may rain in the plains. With food and shoes, it is favorable to go through the mountains." The path is there, whether or not you follow it. Asking the *I Ching* for advice does not commit you to anything but helps you choose with as much information as possible.

Asking a question of the *I Ching* comes down to putting into words a choice that we cannot make. That is why one is well advised to write the question down first, before casting the hexagram. This is not always as easy as it may seem, but it enables one to avoid some mistakes, such as the types of false choices that are formulated as an alternative: "Should I go to the capital or not?"

If you formulate your question in this way you do not rely on yourself but put your fate in the hands of someone else, so that he or she may choose in your stead. This is not the attitude of a Confucian. A Confucian would determine the *goal* first, and then consult the *I Ching* to find out how to *attain* it. And when one is in the midst of alternatives, the indecision can be broken by the use of the double question. Choose one possibility (go to the capital) and ask the *I Ching* about it. You can then complete your information by asking a second question on the opposite alternative (not go to the capital, or, perhaps, stay here) and comparing the two answers. Independent of the answer, this way of proceeding, using a double question, is enriching by itself. Choosing this way of questioning the *I Ching* comes down to answering your own question, because your unconscious desire speaks out: one almost always starts with the choice that is secretly preferred.

This manner of presenting two alternatives originates in a particularity of the Chinese language: the absence of an interrogative form. To ask a question in Chinese, one just mentions, one after the other, the two possibilities that are implicit in the question. "Should I go to the capital" in Chinese is, word for word, "Me go/not go to (the) capital?" (*wo ch'ü pu ch'ü t'ao shou tu*). The answer to this question repeats the verb that was used in the original question, accompanied by the negative particle *pu* if the answer is negative (*ch'ü,* or *pu ch'ü*). This eccentricity can be followed back to the ancient divinatory practices. On one side of the tortoise shell was a series of burnings that was made in regard to the affirmative (do this), and on the other side was a series made about the opposite (do not do this). The tortoise eliminated what was inapplicable, in a way.

THE *I Ching*'s Answer

To a question containing a verb of action, the *I Ching* replies with a verb of action: the name of the hexagram. Unfortunately, most translations hide this logical coherence. This is due to another particularity of Chinese words: they can be either verbs, nouns, adjectives, or adverbs, depending on the context. While an English word often, but not always, has an ending or beginning that indicates its part of speech (such as happy, happiness, happily; open, reopen), Chinese words do not have this variation. But for some reason, most translators have chosen nouns rather than verbs to name hexagrams, which is unfortunate. The entire text loses a great deal of its original energy and becomes simply a catalog of ideas that inspire more intellectual speculation than personal action; this is the difference between naming the thirty-second hexagram Duration, as in the Wilhelm translation, and calling it Lasting. This verbal form, especially in English with the -ing form, which can function both as a verb and as a noun, gives it a more dynamic character and also opens up the possibility of multiple interpretation, as in Chinese. The name of the hexagram greatly influences the interpretation of its following texts and leads the questioner to view the result of the question in a much different light.

"One can be divided into two," said Mao Tse-tung, bringing up to date the ancient dialectical principle of his ancestors. The names of the hexagrams follow this ancient tenet to the letter. They are both *descriptions of situations* (nouns) and *strategies for handling them* (verbs of action). Hexagram 4, Learning How to Learn, describes both the trials and tribulations of early life and the manner in which a "young fool" should be educated. By keeping in mind only the more commonly translated name of the hexagram, Young Fool or Youthful Folly, only one of these two viewpoints is present, and the intended message might be misinterpreted. Or one might worry when a hexagram such as number 6 is cast, whose name is habitually translated as "Conflict." Only in our Western languages does this name suggest a situation that is obstructed. Its reality, in Chinese, is entirely different. It is not Conflict but Resolving the Conflict. It shows the six amicable ways to settle a conflict without going as far as a brutal resolution of the situation, the "state of war" that is represented by the following hexagram, number 7, Organizing Oneself (often named The Army).

Following the name of the hexagram, the *I Ching* deepens its answer with other texts. For example, the positive sense of moderation that runs through the hexagram Resolving the Conflict is clearly presented in the Judgment, where it says,

> Correct/In the middle
> Opening
> At the end
> Obstruction

The Judgment gives an overall commentary on the hexagram. It often comes directly from the oracle bones and is sometimes laconic, "Persistence is beneficial" (no. 34); sometimes explicit, "Bitter Fitting In portends impossibility" (no. 60); sometimes symbolic, "Should the fox get his tail wet just before having finished crossing/No place is beneficial" (no. 64). One can sum up by saying that the Judgment tells what the *I Ching* thinks about the overall situation that is described in the hexagram.

During the Han dynasty, the Judgment was amended by adding a commentary known as the Great Image. The text of the Great Image is much more direct than that of the Judgment. It shows what the *chün tzu* (see note p. 124), the ideal Confucian, should do to have the appropriate attitude for the situation described in the hexagram. Its advice is sometimes moral, "By controlling his thoughts the skillful person does not go beyond the situation" (no. 52); sometimes practical, "By eating and drinking, the skillful person strengthens himself by rest, pleasure, and joy" (no. 5); sometimes about social issues, "By reflecting on the reasons for the trial, the skillful person stays execution" (no. 61). The Great Image often gives advice about individual actions, "By learning and watching over himself, the skillful person enlightens his conduct" (no. 35), and sometimes for groups, "Thanks to the friendship of his companions, the skillful person deliberates to iron out problems, and works with others" (no. 58).

These two texts, the Judgment and the Great Image, make up the first level of the *I Ching*'s answer. At this point there is nothing to distinguish it from a common form of divination, still used in Taiwan and Japan, where a series of bamboo sticks are shaken inside a type of can, and the one that comes out farthest contains the oracle. The second level, which is made up of the Line Texts that accompany each of the hexagram's six lines, reveals a much greater complexity and richness through the direct application of the *I Ching*'s internal mechanisms.

THE CHANGES OF THE LINES

We have already seen, in the first chapter, that each of the lines of the hexagrams is animated by the pendulum-like movement of yin/yang. They are therefore constantly stretching toward their opposites following the rhythm of the Great Reversion. But this rhythm is not regular, it is alive. Between each of the changes, which are characterized by their suddenness, there is a long period of development. The particularity of the chance procedures used when casting a hexagram, either with yarrow stalks or with coins, enables one to determine precisely where each of the lines of the answering hexagram is located, at the moment of the question, within this perpetual motion.

Let us imagine that when casting the *I Ching* a line is selected just after it has changed. A fairly long time will pass during which this line will retain the form, either broken or solid, into which it has just changed. This kind of line, which the Chinese call a young line, is often called a stable or unchanging line. These names are graphic, but they are entirely inappropriate. Nothing in the *I Ching* is stable; if there were no changes, there would be no Book of Changes. This type of line seems stable only because it is still far from the point where it will change. It would be better described as a "lasting" line. Let us now imagine that the line chosen had been just about to change at the time it was chosen. Having reached the culmination of the preceding cycle, it is about to change its nature and is called a changing line. The Chinese prefer to talk about "old" lines. *Old* has two meanings in Chinese: the first highlights what is about to go through an important transformation, and the second is the equivalent of the word *venerable* and is used to describe anyone who should be listened to. These two meanings apply equally well to changing lines. They show that a culmination is approaching, that a reversal of energy is imminent. Because of this, these lines also play a more important part in the interpretation of the answer than the other lines of the hexagram; it is necessary to listen carefully to the advice they give.

The hexagram that is cast shows the energetic organization of the questioner in relation to the question that is in his or her mind at the time. Within this overall link, the presence and position of any changing lines allow the questioner to get more precise information about the answer given. Since the changing lines depend entirely on the random actions of the questioner, they emphasize certain moments in the sequence of events shown in the hexagram and personalize the answer. If two people were to cast the same hexagram, that would mean that at that precise moment, they were in the same situation. But there are many ways to share a situation, that is, sixty-four different arrangements of from zero to six changing lines distributed among six different positions. These distinctive links show the specific relationship that each of the two people has with the hexagram in its overall system.

The additional details given in the Line Texts add to the answer that was started in the Judgment and the Great Image. They refine the overall meaning of the answer according to their position in the hexagram. They show where one is in the hexagram's overall sequence of events. There is a difference in being at the beginning of Overwhelming (no. 55) or at its end. It is not the same to cast Revitalizing Communication (no. 48) and find oneself at the top, where the water is "fresh and cool" (fifth line), as it is to be at the bottom, where it is "muddy" (first line).

Sometimes the text of a particular line may contradict the advice given in the Judgment. This is not an error of logic but an example of the subtlety of the dialectical system of the *I Ching*. In life there are moments where one must go against the flow. These structural details give us a glimpse of the subtle relationship between the hexagrams and their texts. They alone would have earned a reputation of wisdom for the Duke of Chou, who is credited with the writing of the Line Texts. But the system of changing lines does something even more interesting: it creates the hexagram of Perspective.

The 4096 Possible Perspectives

We have seen how a changing line can be drawn at the moment just before it changes. But how, wondered the ancient Chinese, would things be at the moment just after this change? There was no need to burn a tortoise shell to find out; in order to antici-

The hexagram Retreating contains an important lesson in strategy. It shows the situation when only a moment of retreat allows one to prevail over the opposing forces. The difference between retreat and defeat is that retreat is decided according to the circumstances and is not imposed by the enemy. It is a calculated movement that is strategic and offensive in the long term.

In this figure the enemy is represented by the two yin lines that are advancing toward the group of four yang lines that are backing away. The overall advice given by the hexagram is similar to that which would be given to a judoist in a similar situation: let go, give up ground, in order to take advantage of the enemy's attack to make him fall. But at the second line it says, "Hold back stubbornly, like the skin of a yellow steer. Nothing can make one let go." Why at this stage of retreating should one hold one's ground? The second line marks the transition point between the yin lines and the yang lines. In order to retreat properly, one needs to avoid being overrun by the opposing troops. It is necessary for a group of soldiers to "keep in contact with the enemy," as the official manuals say. To achieve effectively what the hexagram is advising, that is, giving up ground, and to favor the general retreating movement of the four yang lines, it is essential that at the second line the contrary is performed: holding ground and attacking head-on. Not too strong, just enough for the enemy to have to protect himself, to get organized for a counterattack, and so on. This allows time for those who are delayed to catch up to the rest of the lines, which are retreating properly (the second line changes and becomes yang). The thirty-third hexagram teaches us that a well-organized retreat is made up of a main movement of retreat and a secondary movement of resistance.

pate this immediate future, all that is necessary is to make this change happen, by transforming each of the changing lines of the hexagram to their opposites. In this manner one obtains what I call the hexagram of Perspective.

This hexagram "to come" gives us information about the probable evolution of the situation that is described in the hexagram that has been cast. The Chinese call these two figures the root hexagram and the bud hexagram. They are interconnected by a relationship that is less contingent than our idea of cause and effect, because the eventuality of this second figure depends neither on the mechanical laws of causality nor on the vague decrees of fate. The materialization of this future, contained in the present situation as a seed, depends entirely on the questioner's free will to follow the *I Ching*'s advice or not. The appearance of this second hexagram radically changes our perspective on the use of the *I Ching* as a divinatory tool and shows its astonishing internal complexity. In contrast to divination, which imposes an obligatory order on events, which will "come true," the system of the *I Ching* merely suggests possible futures that depend only on us. The *I Ching* shows us an authentic world, in all its complexity; it is up to us to find the path, chosen from the many available, that leads where we want to go.

Because of the changing lines, any hexagram can change into any of the sixty-three others, or all sixty-four could "remain the same," because of the possibility of there being no changing lines.[2] In that case the figure is called stable, but to use that term would be to make the same mistake as when discussing the changing lines. The hexagram actually changes into itself, somewhat like an old-fashioned record that is scratched and repeats the same thing. It is a lasting hexagram. Casting the *I Ching* does not, therefore, present a choice among sixty-four possible answers, but rather 64×64 couples of hexagrams, or 4096 possible developments, all different and all significant. Let us look at some examples. In the box on page oo there is a discussion of strategic withdrawal. But where does this withdrawal lead us? Toward Progressing Step by Step (no. 53), when the fourth line changes; toward Overcoming What Causes Obstruction (no. 39), when the fourth and sixth lines change; toward Bursting (no. 43), when the first, second, and sixth lines change, and so on.

Here one can get a glimpse of the elegance and precision of the answers given by the *I Ching*. All this comes from the complexity of its inner workings, which combine the mantic texts from tortoise shells with the linear relationships that link the hexagrams among themselves. Hexagram 52, Stabilizing, talks about learning to be stable and having self-control. But the Line Text for the third line describes, to the contrary, a moment when "the heart suffocates," a moment of extreme tension[3] within an overall process of stabilization. Why did the Duke of Chou (or those that he represents) put this text at the third line of this hexagram? Perhaps it is because when this line changes it makes hexagram 23 appear, whose name, Enduring, signifies that we must fight against getting worn out.

This one example among 384 others (64×6) shows the close relationship between the Line Text and the hexagram that appears when the line changes. It connects the two sides of the *I Ching,* which are usually seen as opposites in the West: the beautifully logical arrangement of the hexagrams and the irrational disorder of the divinatory texts. However, the two are connected by a deep structural link, which may be what enabled the Chou diviners to organize the tortoise shell texts. But this link can only be seen through the system of changes, and therefore, only when the *I Ching* is used for divinatory purposes. This is why it has been overlooked for so long.

The *I Ching* is impenetrable only to those who do not dare open the book; the key to its logical structure is under the doormat of divination. But to use it, one must discover the combination that opens the lock of chance.

4

From Chance to Coupling

Chance is the dark side of our lives. Everyone comes across it, but no one can explain it. It is a shadow on our mental logic; it is rejected, denied, and even its very definition is negative: it is the absence of order. Since it is difficult to reflect on that which does not exist, most of us prefer to avoid a direct encounter with chance. Two attitudes result from this, both of them extreme and paradoxical, because they are both based on the same denial that an absence of order may exist. Those who believe in chance do so by calling it an underlying order that is not a result of causality; those who deny it call it a causal order that has not yet been explained. Between these two bastions there is no reasonable middle ground. How can one then justify using the Book of Changes, when its validity is proven, by the precision of its advice, each time a question is asked? The idea that one might make decisions by tossing a coin seems to us, unconsciously, like abandoning reason. But in China, it is just the opposite.

The Chinese are not afraid of chance. It has always seemed to them to be the best way to link themselves with the ever-changing flow of yin/yang. But do the Chinese mean the same thing as we do when they speak of *chance*?

How Do You Say *Chance* in Chinese?

The best way to find the meaning of a word in a foreign language is to look in a dictionary. If you look for the word *chance* in an English-Chinese dictionary, you will find two characters, *ou* and *p'eng*. But to be certain that these words are really talking about chance as we understand it, especially in a civilization so different from ours, you need to do the opposite: look up all of the meanings of these two characters in a Chinese-English dictionary. Suddenly everything is a bit less clear. Among the common meanings for *ou* and *p'eng*, those for chance as we understand it are found at the end of the list, which shows that they are of very recent usage. And, it seems, they are used essentially to translate terms from foreign languages. The main meanings for these two words, however, are: "even," "equal," "coupling"; "association," "linking."

The traditional symbol of chance in our society is the flip of a coin. This may be one of the reasons that the casting of a hexagram with coins is more or less unconsciously deprecated in our minds. But even worse, the Chinese would say that our image of chance is incomplete. A coin cannot stay in the air forever; it must eventually fall to the ground, landing on one side or the other. It is as if the difficulty we have in conceiving of the idea of chance has caused us to choose, as its symbol, an impossible situation: the coin *in* the air. The Chinese do not see things in the same way. They think the most important moment is when the coin lands, because it is only then that we can discover the quality of the moment and adapt ourselves to it in the best possible manner. For them, the symbol of chance is not an inanimate object but a beautiful animal, the oriole, chosen for the elegant way it lands.

Birds are the animals that are the least governed by terrestrial influences. The flight of these messengers from heaven is totally free. The genius of the Chinese was to have chosen this image of freedom as the symbol of perfect union with the moment. Orioles fly where they want to and land where they want. With this freedom they always land where they should; in other words, at the place where their union with the situation is the most appropriate. This is why they are masters worthy of imitation by human beings. "The golden oriole knows his place when he sings." Confucius asked, in a comment on this sentence from the Book of Poetry, "Is it possible that a human being could know less than this bird?" The *I Ching*'s role is to teach us to do what birds do naturally. Now we can see why the Chinese concept of chance is entirely different from ours. Perhaps the best way to discover exactly what we think of chance would be to look at the word itself.

A ROLL OF THE DICE

Dice are the oldest gaming objects known and represent the earliest attempts to tame chance and use it for a definite purpose. Although Sophocles and Herodotus each give accounts of their creation, the former by a Greek and the latter by a Lydian, it has been found that dice go much further back in time. They have been found in Egyptian tombs dating back to 2000 BCE, and have been used by peoples on every populated continent. Their original purpose was just that of the *I Ching*: divination. Yet they later became simple toys, and their divinatory system fell into disuse.

What else do dice have to do with the *I Ching*? Nothing directly, but they are present in the original meaning of the word *chance* in English. *Chance*, like so many other words, comes from French. In spite of the many wars between the French and the English in the Middle Ages, the two languages became so intricately intertwined that it is sometimes difficult to tell whether a word went from French to English or vice versa. Thousands of French words make up our daily vocabulary, and *chance* is one of the more common ones. It comes from the Old French *chéance*, which meant "the way the dice fall." Oddly enough, these dice come up often in the investigation of *chance*, because the more "learned" word for this concept, *aleatory*, comes from the Latin *alea*, which also means dice. And our word *die*, or *dice*, comes, again, from the French word *dé*, which in turn comes from the Latin *datum*, which can mean gifts, or fate (what the gods have given). This word *datum* also gives us the word *date*, which is a way of freezing the moment and inscribing its characteristics: its day and time.

The word *chance*, or its French predecessor, is also related to another French word, *choir*, which means to fall. Another related word is *cadence*, which is a musical rhythm. The Latin word that gave rise to both of these words is *cadere*, which means to fall.

This word, combined with the preposition *ad,* gives us *accido,* which is later our *accident.*

This detour gives us an idea of the semantic map that underlies our idea of chance, and its evolution, and shows us how ingrained the concept of chance is in our psyche. The concept talks about something that falls, and more specifically dice, which have a way of freezing the moment; it talks about fate, what is given by the gods, that is, the powers outside of our control; it talks about rhythm, regularity; and it talks about accidents, things that happen unexpectedly. All of these ideas are present in the *I Ching.* Showing us the characteristics of the frozen moment is the main goal of the *I Ching.* To be in contact with powers beyond our control: is that not why we consult the *I Ching?* The rhythm of nature and the Tao, these are also important concepts in the *I Ching.* The goal of the *I Ching* is to fit one's actions into the rhythm of the primal forces, and these concepts come up in our investigation of the word *chance* and its derivatives. Yet for some reason, there is still a difference in the way we perceive these concepts.

It may be that the difference resides in the word *accident,* which means anything that happens, especially by chance. While this word is inherently negative in our subconscious, it is not always so; you meet someone *by accident,* but this could be a very good opportunity. But somewhere along the line this concept of chance took on the negative connotations that color it in our mind.

Our attitude is reflected in Albert Einstein's comment that "God does not play dice." This is a way of saying that there is no room for chance in a deterministic world, and it is particularly telling that Einstein chose the image of dice to represent chance. The existence of an omnipotent God, who is the creator of the universe, logically precludes the possibility that chance may play a role in the game of life. But in an absolute manner, this creator also precludes the possibility of free will. Fate, the hand of God, guides us through our existence.

The Chinese, on the other hand, have no Creator. The very concept is so foreign to them that missionaries have always had trouble translating the words *God* and *Creator* into Chinese. For them, this absolutely deterministic world cannot exist, and there is no reason why free will cannot be influenced by chance. After all, the *I Ching* does not dictate actions, it only gives advice. You are free to choose to follow that advice or not.

Nature, like God, is omnipotent. It determines what will happen in advance according to its proper laws, but, unlike God, it is not inscrutable. As soon as its laws are known, the future can be predicted and

chance can be beaten. Cartesian rationalism established this position by rejecting that which did not fit
into the rational world: chance and faith. Blaise Pas-
cal, the mystical mathematician, showed how to get
around chance by calculating probabilities. Then Jo-
hannes Kepler and Isaac Newton confirmed the tri-
umph of determinism by taking the seemingly erratic
movements of the planets and reducing them to
equations. Finally Einstein, the last great scientist of
the classical age, when confronted with the limits of
his theories, could not let go of his heritage. In a
letter to Max Born, he said, "You believe in [a] God
who plays dice, and I in complete law and order in a
world which objectively exists."[1] Almost one century
later, chaos theory has taught us that he was looking
at the problem from the wrong side: it is chance that
is playing God.

CHAOS THEORY

Chaos was the name of the monstrous confusion that
the universe was plunged into before the Greeks
came and straightened it out. This word has remained in our language, with the meaning of total
disorder or the dissolution of social or physical laws.
It is now the name of one of the most fantastic intellectual advances of this century: the theory of deter-

minist chaos. The list of fields to which chaos theory has brought new ways of thinking is long and is still growing: astronomy, mechanics, electronics, optics, acoustics, fluid mechanics, biology, medicine, geophysics, consciousness studies. In fact, this theory is developing tools capable of clearing up issues regarding a number of daily phenomena that had previously been left aside by classical science as exceptions to Cartesian causality.

The determinist point of view has always stumbled over the manifestations of chance. Even though the physical laws that govern the toss of a dice are known perfectly, it is impossible to predict which side will show when it settles. To get out of this tight spot, probabilities are calculated that simply enable one to have an idea of the percentage of chance that one side or another will show. There was thus an opposition between determinist systems on one side and aleatory systems on another: science and its dark side. Between the two there was nothing, until chaos theory came along and suddenly showed that there are systems that are both determinist and aleatory.

Just as with the Shang diviners, it was a question about the clouds in the sky that brought about this discovery. Up until the 1960s, it was believed that the paucity of accurate results obtained by meteorological prediction was due to the complexity of the interactions that took place in the atmosphere. But at MIT the young meteorologist Edward Lorenz was not convinced by this idea. "Lorenz enjoyed weather. . . . He savored its changeability. He appreciated the patterns that come and go in the atmosphere."[2] One day he decided to get to the bottom of the complexity of weather forecasting by inventing a model of atmospheric circulation that was governed in a simple and deterministic way by three equations with three unknowns. To his surprise he discovered that his system was not deterministic. Slight variations in the initial conditions brought about erratic and diverging results. Complexity was not the question, it was an intrinsic property of the system itself. Even though it is governed by known, determinist laws, the atmosphere eludes determinism: it is chaotic. Edward Lorenz called this characteristic, whose technical name is "sensitive dependence on initial conditions," the butterfly effect. This postulates that the wind created by a butterfly's wings in the China Sea could cause a tornado in America.

Edward Lorenz's discoveries inspired others in the world of science and soon became important. In 1971 David Ruelle and Boris Takens, at the Institut des Hautes Études Scientifiques, in France, noticed that when shown graphically, chaotic systems seemed to be attracted to specific areas in space, which they named "strange attractors." They said, "Strange attractors and fractals evoke a deep memory that comes close to the convoluted and entangled images of Celtic art from the Bronze Age, the complex shapes of Shang dynasty ritual vases, the visual patterns of the Indians from the West Coast of America, the myths of labyrinths and mazes, the iterated language games of children, or the rhythms of the songs of so-called primitive peoples."[3]

If the state of a chaotic system at a given moment is found to be at some point along its strange attractor, it will be found, later on in its trajectory, at some other point along the attractor. But it is impossible to predict exactly where and when. Yet the attractor is still the same, it only depends on the physical characteristics of the system. If it does not change, then why is its evolution unpredictable? Because strange attractors do not answer to the usual criteria of geometry. They are infinite curves, that is, they are infinitely detailed, a property that is called, in scientific terms, scaling symmetry, or self-similarity. This property can be seen on boxes of cocoa sold in France in the 1930s, under the name Banania. On the cover of the box was a picture of an African Zouave holding up a box of Banania in his hand, on which was a picture of a Zouave holding up a box of Banania, on which . . . The system formed by this image is self-similar: at each level the entire structure and all the information about the system can be found. This type of image has no beginning or scale; it is a fractal. Fractals are seen not only in strange attractors; in fact they are among the most common properties in nature. The veins of leaves imitate the structure of branches, and the rivulets of water on the beach form the same types of patterns as blood vessels in the hand. This is probably why fractal geometry has no equal when it comes to imitating the irregular, complex shapes of nature and the movement of life.

And this may be what chaos theory has in common with the *I Ching*. Hexagrams, which are a blend of chance and determinism, also represent the continual evolution of a system, and yet they are of no help at all in predicting its evolution. But what hexagrams have most in common with strange attractors is one essential quality: self-similarity. A hexagram is only a sort of "freeze-frame," a characteristic combination of yin and yang lines in continual change. If only one of the lines changes, a new hexagram appears. The hexagram that results from this change, called the derived hexagram, is traditionally said in China to "live within" the line that makes it appear during a change. This is the poetic description of a perfectly self-similar organization. At each of the lines of a hexagram resides another whole hexagram. And at each of this new hexagram is another new hexagram, and so on. The overall structure of the *I Ching* can be found at each point within the system: hexagrams have no scale.

The situations dealt with by hexagrams have no scale either, since any anecdotal aspect of the situation is glossed over by a systemic and dynamic view of it. For the Chinese mind, symmetry of scale is an obvious fact that extends to the very structure of all organisms, whether they are cities, plants, countries, or human beings. Books on Chinese medicine use political metaphors to talk about organic functions (the spleen is said to have a role in the body similar to that of the head of the army), and the *I Ching* uses bodily metaphors to present different stages of situations of incitation (hexagram 31) or stabilization (hexagram 52). It is this very ability of the Chinese to go directly to the deep structure without looking at details that enables the *I Ching* to function so far from its originating civilization.

The Chinese concept of chance, which gives the *I Ching* its validity, has found its echo in chaos theory. The concepts presented by this theory give us vital information about how the *I Ching* functions. Understanding this may help us cross the bridge between determinist rationality and chance, and go further toward our comprehension of this age-old system, which could have a profound influence on the rest of our lives.

Conclusion

When the Marquis of Tai left for his long journey into the hereafter, did he know that the *I Ching* would make an even longer journey on earth? Probably not, because he would have really needed to be a diviner to imagine the interest that this book would hold for the rest of the world.

In the past couple of generations, Chinese civilization has taken a place in our culture. Acupuncture, *chi kung,* and chop suey are no longer exotic words but realities of daily life, and no one is surprised to see the drawing of the Great Reversion (see p. 11) used as a logo by so many surfers. But this alone cannot explain why the *I Ching* is so appreciated in the West. After all, Yoga has also become commonplace, but the Ramayana has not become a best-seller.

We are living in a period of change, and Yoga is part of this movement that seeks new ways of looking at our bodies and our minds. But the *I Ching* is different from such a physical or spiritual technique; it is a dialog.

The *I Ching* speaks to us so directly that we tend to forget the strangest thing about it: that it does speak to us. This is no miracle; the old Classic of Changes speaks to us because we ask it to. We are the ones who give it this capability. The *I Ching* is not a book that is read from beginning to end but one that we consult when we need to. For many years people thought it was just a book of divination. If that were the case, the *I Ching* would deserve to remain forever on the shelves of New Age bookstores. Also, if that were true, the Chinese would have rejected it long ago for being inefficient, just as they are now doing for their centrally planned economy.

The Chinese are also living in a period of important changes. But it seems that they know how to deal with this better than we do, as if change were something they have known for as long as they have known the *I Ching*. For them, as for us, the Book of Changes speaks, both elusively and dynamically, about what each one is experiencing. But to us Westerners it gives something more: the art of managing change. Our culture is based on stability. The Hebrews taught us about the existence of an eternal God; Plato taught us about the existence of absolute ideas; Descartes taught us about intangible physical laws. But no one has taught us what to do when confronted with change.

That is why the *I Ching* has been discovered in the West at just the right time. It brings us a new point of view that widens our perspective. By translating everything that is factual in the changing situations that we experience into a drawing of its energies, with changing lines highlighting the tensions that our own involvement provokes, the *I Ching*'s answers give us new reference points and suggest new strategies. And in doing so, it speaks so naturally that we almost forget that it has come to us across millennia and oceans.

But the *I Ching* still has its exotic side: its form, its figures, its text, the raw poetry that it exudes, and the images that it uses are all surprising when we first encounter them. Then, little by little, its universe starts resonating with our own. The distinctive perspective of the *I Ching*, that aerial view of our inner landscape, becomes familiar to us. We discover the language of change.

When you learn a foreign language you never forget your mother tongue. Learning another way to approach daily situations does not make us forget how we have always done so. Both of these can widen our minds. The *I Ching*, a typically Chinese invention, has become one of humankind's treasures, not only because the ancient Chinese had a stroke of genius that inspired them to invent a binary alphabet of solid and broken lines and use it to represent the movements of life, but also because the ideal that it puts forth, the *chün tzu,* the Confucian gentleman (see p. ooo), does not conflict with any religious ideals. The "gentleman" is not a superman, he is only someone who has learned, thanks to his familiarity with the *I Ching,* to do the right thing at the right time, to make any situation as productive as possible. The *I Ching,* which is a book of strategy for daily living, is more than just a means for reflecting on the changes underlying this life: it suggests a responsible way to fit into it.

Taking your fate in your own hands, not giving in to the ungraspable Tao, but following its tracks, observing it, learning its ebb and flow in order to find the best way to be in harmony with it, like surfing a wave—perhaps this is the most important lesson the *I Ching* has to give us.

By giving us the means to lead our lives through the obstacles that it encounters, the *I Ching* increases our freedom and all human dignity with it. But it goes even further. Through its marriage of chance and necessity it shows, as does chaos theory, that life is neither predictable nor erratic but is a harmonious combination of the two. The future is both controlled in general and unpredictable in its particularities.

The Marquis of Tai knew this when he took his precious silk scrolls into the hereafter. But if he valued them so much, perhaps it is because he knew that the Book of Changes' objective is eternal: to help each human being find their place in the great vital movement that flows through them; to play their part on the great stage of heaven/earth; in short, to be the coauthor of their own fate.

Appendix: Names of the Sixty-Four Hexagrams

Notes

Translator's Preface

1. Centre Djohi, Association pour l'étude et l'usage du Yi Jing, BP 322, 75229 Paris Cedex 05, France. Website: http://www.mcelhearn.com/yijing. By e-mail: kirk@mcelhearn.com.
2. Cyrille Javary, *Yi Jing Jing Yi, etude sur l'origine du Yi Jing* (Rennes: Cercle Sinologique de l'Ouest, 1985).

Introduction

1. All translations from the *I Ching* are by the author.
2. *Encyclopedia Britannica,* 15th ed. (1990), 6:209.
3. I. M. Pei, "Discours de réception à l'Académie" (Paris: Palais de l'Institut, 1984).
4. François Jacob, "Analyse des modèles linguistiques en biologie," *Critique* (1974).
5. Fritjof Capra, *The Tao of Physics* (Boston: Shambhala Publications, 1983).
6. C. G. Jung, *Synchronicity: An Acausal Connecting Principle* (Princeton: Princeton University Press, 1973).

Chapter 1. Hexagrams and Holograms

1. The core text is the oldest layer of text of the *I Ching,* which includes texts known as the Judgments and the texts pertaining to each line of each hexagram. The Great Images and the additional commentaries are all later additions.

2. The largest-selling daily newspaper in China, and the official organ of the Chinese Communist Party.
3. Li Xiao Lung (Bruce Lee), *Chuan Dao Shun Tung Fa,* volume 8, Hong Kong.
4. As the Grateful Dead song suggests, "the faster we go, the rounder we get."
5. After a drawing by Jean Marolleau.
6. *Koan* is the Japanese transcription of the Chinese character that names hexagram 20, Seeing the Truth.

Chapter 2. From Bronze to Opium

1. Claude Larre, *Les Chinois* (Paris: Lidis-Brepols, 1982).
2. Léon Vandermeersch, "De la tortue à l'achillée" in *Divination et rationalité* (Paris: Le Seuil, 1974).
3. Ibid.
4. The term *superior man* used by Richard Wilhelm and others is somewhat misleading. The Chinese term *chün tzu* contains no implication of superiority, in the sense of being better than others or above others. The *chün-tzu* is rather the person who can act in accordance with the laws of the universe. The term *gentleman* might express part of that idea, but in its archaic sense, that of one who is a "person of distinction" or "of chivalrous instincts and fine feelings" (*Shorter Oxford English Dictionary*). The concept of chivalry itself is very close to what the ideal of the *chün-tzu* was: "the character of the ideal knight; disinterested bravery, honor, and courtesy" (*Shorter Oxford*). The *chün-tzu* is a noble person not by virtue of birth but by having a noble heart. An appropriate English term might be *skillful person,* in the Buddhist sense of one who uses skillful means.
5. *Tao-te Ching,* chapter 25.
6. Marcel Granet, *La Pensée Chinoise* (Paris: Albin Michel, 1968).
7. M. I. Bergeron, *Wang Pi, philosophe du non-avoir* (Paris: Institut Ricci, 1986).

8. Ibid.
9. Richard Wilhelm, *The I Ching,* trans. Cary F. Baynes (Princeton: Princeton University Press, 1950).
10. Alain Daniélou, *Les Chemins du labyrinthe* (Paris: Robert Laffont, 1981).

Chapter 3. Yarrow Stalks, Coins, and Tea Leaves

1. *Random House Dictionary of the English Language,* 2d ed. (New York: Random House, 1987).
2. In fact, this is the case approximately 17 percent of the time.
3. As Ralph Kramden would say, "Pins and needles, needles and pins, a happy man is a man who grins."

Chapter 4 From Chance to Coupling

1. I. Born, trans., *The Born-Einstein Letters, Sept. 7, 1944* (New York: Macmillan, 1971).
2. James Gleick, *Chaos, the Making of a New Science* (New York: Viking, 1987).
3. John Briggs and David Peat, *Turbulent Mirror: An Illustrated Guide to Chaos Theory and the Science of Wholeness* (New York: Harper & Row, 1989).

Glossary

BOOK OF CHANGES. The common name for the *I Ching* in English. It is more correct to call it the Classic of Changes.

CHING. A classic. See box p. xii.

CHOU. Name of the third Chinese dynasty, which ruled from the twelfth to the third century BCE.

CHOU I. The name commonly used by the Chinese for the *I Ching*. It means the Chou Changes, or the Book of Changes of the Chou Dynasty.

CHOU KUNG. The Duke of Chou. The younger brother of King Wen. He acted as regent from the death of his brother until his nephew was of age to take the throne. The legend says that he wrote the Line Texts in order to educate his nephew. As an ideal example of a ruling sage, he was one of Confucius's preferred role models. Confucius once exclaimed, in a moment of discouragement, "It has been a long time since I last saw the Duke of Chou in a dream" (*Analects,* chapter 6, §5).

CHU HSI. Chinese philosopher whose work on the *I Ching* has been used as the basis for all official Chinese studies of it, as well as for almost all its translations.

FIVE CLASSICS (Wu Ching). The traditional name given to the five key texts of the Confucian school. Most of these texts were established during the Han dynasty. They are the *I Ching*, the *Shih Ching,* the Classic of Poetry; the *Shu Ching,* the Classic of History; the *Ch'un Ch'iu,* the Spring and Autumn Annals; and the *Li Chi,* the Collection of Rituals.

FU HSI (pronounced Foo Shee). The legendary figure to whom

is attributed the "discovery" of the trigrams. The Great Commentary says about him, "Raising his head, he contemplated the figures in the heavens. Lowering his head, he contemplated the shapes on the ground. All around him, he contemplated the signs of the birds and the animals and the way they adapted to different lands. Proceeding directly from all of the parts of the body, and indirectly from the ten thousand living things, he organized the eight figures that made it possible to classify the ten thousand beings according to their nature and to be in harmony with the force of light that animates them" (Great Commentary, Part 2, chapter 2, §1). Fu Hsi is often shown covered with leaves, emerging from within a mountain, holding a brush in the hand that had just drawn the trigrams (usually shown in the King Wen order). Legend has it that he was born near the city of T'ien-shui, in the Kansu region, in the northwest of China. Every year, on the fifth day of the fifth month, great festivals are organized to celebrate his birthday.

GREAT COMMENTARY. This important text makes up the fifth and sixth wings of the canonical commentaries. Probably written around the fourth century BCE, it is a set of global thoughts about the *I Ching* and its inherent worldview. This text contains the first examples of the terms *yin* and *yang* used with their philosophical meanings.

GREAT IMAGES. The traditional name for the third and fourth wings of the canonical commentaries. Written during the Han dynasty, these Confucian commentaries follow a regular structure: first a description of the hexagram according to the trigrams that compose it, then a description of the most appropriate attitude to adopt according to the overall situation.

HAN. Name of the fourth Chinese dynasty, which ruled from 206 BCE to 220 CE. During this reign the *I Ching* as we know it was organized and established.

HEXAGRAM. One of the sixty-four figures of the *I Ching*, made up of six lines. *Kua* in Chinese.

HUANG TI. The Yellow Emperor. A legendary figure, Huang
   Ti is essentially a practical genius. He organized government,
   systematized the different types of writing, founded mathematics, and reflected on numbers, music, and industrial tech-
   niques. All books about acupuncture claim his patronage, as
   do works of Taoism.

JUDGMENT. The name traditionally given to the paragraphs
   that begin each of the sixty-four chapters of the *I Ching*. Legend credits King Wen with their composition. These texts are
   summaries of the Shang diviners' experiences and descend
   directly from the mantic texts engraved on tortoise shells. In
   a practical sense, they give an overall description of the situation described by the hexagram.

KING WEN. See Wen Wang.

KUA. The general name given to all the figures of the *I Ching*. It
   means an organized collection of divinatory information and
   is applied without distinction to hexagrams, trigrams, and bigrams.

LINE TEXTS (*yao tz'u*). *Yao* is the technical name for the lines
   of the hexagrams, and the character itself represents the
   cracks on tortoise shells. *Tz'u* means sentence. There are six
   line texts for each hexagram, that describe the place of each
   line in the overall situation presented in the hexagram.

PA KUA. Literally, "eight divinatory figures," this expression is
   usually translated as "eight trigrams."

SHANG. The name of the second Chinese dynasty, which ruled
   from the eighteenth to the twelfth century BCE.

SHU CHING. The third of the Five Classics, the Classic of History.

TEN WINGS. The traditional name for the canonical commentaries on the *I Ching*. Established during the Han dynasty, they
   are the first and second wings, T'uan-chuan, the Commentary
   on the Decision; the third and fourth wings, Hsiang-chuan,
   the Great Images and the Small Images; the fifth and sixth

wings, Ta-chuan, the Great Commentary; the seventh wing, Wen-yen, the Commentary on the Words; the eighth wing, Shuo-kua, Discussion of the Figures; the ninth wing, Hsü-kua, the Order of the Figures; and the tenth wing, Tsa-kua, the Combined Figures.

TRIGRAM. A set of three lines, each of which may be either solid or broken. There are eight trigrams, and they synthesize the information given in the sixty-four hexagrams. They use images of nature as symbols, such as wind, mountain, rain, sun, and so forth. Each hexagram can be seen as resulting from the combination of two trigrams. From this comes a vivid description of the type of situation represented by the entire hexagram. This allows one to determine a general attitude that is appropriate for the moment in question. The internal attitude is determined by the lower trigram, and the external attitude is determined by the upper trigram. There are two main orders for the trigrams. One of them, called the Early Heaven order, is attributed to Fu Hsi. Although this order is very common in Western books on the *I Ching*, it is hardly ever found in China on "eight trigram mirrors" (*pa kua ching tzu*). These are a small round mirror with the eight trigrams on a wooden frame surrounding it. Such mirrors are supposed to protect their owners from demons, who run away, frightened by their own images. The other order, called the Later Heaven order, is attributed to King Wen (Wen Wang). Seen everywhere in China, it is rarely explained sufficiently in Western books.

WEN WANG. The founding father of the Chou dynasty. This historic king was credited with all the civil virtues of Chinese culture. His name means "writing," "(intellectual) culture," as well as "civilization." The legend of the *I Ching* credits him not only with having created the sixty-four hexagrams by combining Fu Hsi's trigrams in twos, the invention of their names, and the composition of the Judgments, but also with the Later Heaven order for the trigrams.

YARROW. The yarrow is a fernlike plant that grows readily from

Beijing to Boston and is often found in fields or alongside paths. It has flat-topped clusters of whitish flowers and a long straight stalk that grows to about two feet in height. To make your own yarrow stalks for casting the *I Ching*, simply cut enough yarrow flowers, cut the stalks to the desired length, and let them dry for a few days.

Select Bibliography

Blofeld, John, trans. *The Book of Change*. New York: Dutton, 1965.

Cleary, Thomas, trans. *I Ching: The Tao of Organization*. Boston: Shambhala, 1988.

————, trans. *I Ching Mandalas*. Boston: Shambhala, 1989.

————, trans. *The Buddhist I Ching*. Boston: Shambhala, 1987.

————, trans. *The Taoist I Ching*. Boston: Shambhala, 1986.

Dick, Philip K. *The Man in the High Castle*. New York: Vintage, 1962. A science fiction novel about the *I Ching*, written using the *I Ching*.

Huang, Kerson, and Rosemary Huang. *The I Ching*. New York: Workman, 1985.

Huang, Kerson. *I Ching: The Oracle*. Singapore: World Scientific Publishing Co. Pty Ltd., 1984. This is the original version of the above book and is of interest because it contains the Chinese text facing the translations of each hexagram.

The I Ching: An Illustrated Guide to the Chinese Art of Divination. Tan Xiaochun, Illustrator, and Koh Kok Kiang, translator. Singapore: Asiapac Books Pty Ltd, 1993. A comic book version of the *I Ching*.

Jung, C. G. *Synchronicity: An Acausal Connecting Principle*. Translated by R. F. C. Hull. Princeton, N.J.: Princeton University Press, 1960.

Moore, Steve. *The Trigrams of Han: Inner Structures of the I Ching*. London: Aquarian, 1989. For a detailed explanation of the trigrams in the *I Ching*.

Peat, F. David. *Synchronicity: The Bridge between Matter and Mind.* New York: Bantam Books, 1987.

Shchutskii, Iulaim K. *Researches on the I Ching.* Translated by William L. MacDonald, Tsuyoshi Hasegawa, and Hellmut Wilhelm. Princeton, N.J.: Princeton University Press, 1979.

Sui, R. G. *The Portable Dragon: The Western Man's Guide to the I Ching.* Cambridge, Mass.: MIT Press, 1968. This book, rather than trying to be another translation of the *I Ching*, attempts to present the meaning of each hexagram through quotes from different texts.

Smith, Kidder, Jr.; Peter K. Bol; Joseph A. Adler; and Don J. Wyatt. *Sung Dynasty Uses of the I Ching.* Princeton, N.J.: Princeton University Press, 1990.

Wei, Henry. *The Authentic I Ching.* San Bernadino, Cal.: Borgo Press, 1987.

Wei, Tat. *An Exposition of the I Ching or* Book of Changes. Taipei: Institute of Cultural Studies, 1970.

Whincup, Greg. *Rediscovering the I Ching.* New York: Doubleday, 1986.

Wilhelm, Richard, trans. *The I Ching,* or Book of Changes. Translated by C. F. Baynes. Princeton, N.J.: Princeton University Press, 1967.